Windows 11 for Seniors

Mastering the Digital Landscape with Comprehensive and Practical Tutorials | Discover Your Roadmap to Digital Independence

Toni Davison

Windows 11 for Seniors
© Copyright 2023 by Toni Davison
All rights reserved

This document is geared towards providing exact and reliable information with regards to the topic and issue covered. The publication is sold with the idea that the publisher is not required to render accounting, officially permitted, or otherwise, qualified services. If advice is necessary, legal or professional, a practiced individual in the profession should be ordered. From a Declaration of Principles which was accepted and approved equally by a Committee of the American Bar Association and a Committee of Publishers and Associations. In no way is it legal to reproduce, duplicate, or transmit any part of this document in either electronic means or in printed format. Recording of this publication is strictly prohibited and any storage of this document is not allowed unless with written permission from the publisher.

All rights reserved.

The information provided herein is stated to be truthful and consistent, in that any liability, in terms of inattention or otherwise, by any usage or abuse of any policies, processes, or directions contained within is the solitary and utter responsibility of the recipient reader. Under no circumstances will any legal responsibility or blame be held against the publisher for any reparation, damages, or monetary loss due to the information herein, either directly or indirectly. Respective authors own all copyrights not held by the publisher. The information herein is offered for informational purposes solely, and is universal as so. The presentation of the information is without contract or any type of guarantee assurance. The trademarks that are used are without any consent, and the publication of the trademark is without permission or backing by the trademark owner. All trademarks and brands within this book are for clarifying purposes only and are the owned by the owners themselves, not affiliated with this document.

TABLE OF CONTENTS

INTRODUCTION 1

A Brief Overview of Windows 11 1

The Differences Between Windows 11 and Previous Versions 3

Understanding the Windows 11 Interface 6

The Advantages of Upgrading to Windows 11 8

Setting Expectations: What this Book Covers 10

CHAPTER 1: GETTING STARTED WITH WINDOWS 11 13

Installing or Upgrading to Windows 11 13

Navigating the Windows 11 Desktop 15

Understanding Basic Windows 11 Terminology 17

Adjusting Basic System Settings 20

Setting Up User Accounts 22

CHAPTER 2: MASTERING THE CORE FEATURES 25

The Start Menu and Taskbar 25

Working with Apps and Programs 26

Using the File Explorer 28

Customizing the Desktop and Taskbar 30

Using the Action Center and Notifications 32

Using the Clipboard History and Snipping Tool 33

CHAPTER 3: INTERNET AND EMAIL 37

Setting Up Your Internet Connection 37

Navigating the Web with Microsoft Edge 38

Introduction to Email and Setting up Mail 40

Best Practices for Internet Safety 42

Introduction to Search Engines and Online Research 44

Understanding Cookies, Pop-ups, and Ad Blockers 46

CHAPTER 4: COMMUNICATING AND CONNECTING **49**

Understanding Social Media 49

Setting Up and Using Skype 50

Introduction to Microsoft Teams 53

Connecting and Sharing with Other Devices 54

Using Cloud Services for Storage and Sharing 56

CHAPTER 5: PERSONALIZATION AND ACCESSIBILITY **59**

Personalizing Your Desktop 59

Adjusting Accessibility Settings 61

Using Speech Recognition and Cortana 62

Setting Up Printers and Other External Devices 64

Using Windows 11's Ease of Access Features 65

CHAPTER 6: SECURITY AND MAINTENANCE **67**

Understanding Windows 11 Security Features 67

Protecting Your PC from Viruses and Malware 69

Regular System Maintenance and Updates 70

Backing Up and Restoring Your System 72

Troubleshooting Common Issues 73

CHAPTER 7: EXPLORING FURTHER 77

Introduction to Microsoft Office Suite 77

Using Windows Store to Download Apps and Games 78

Basic Photo Editing with Microsoft Photos 79

Enjoying Music and Videos with Media Player 82

Closing Remarks and Next Steps 84

BONUS 1: AUDIOBOOK 87

BONUS 2: VIDEO 89

EXCLUSIVE BONUS: 3 EBOOK 91

AUTHOR BIO: TONI DAVISON 93

Toni Davison

INTRODUCTION

A Brief Overview of Windows 11

Windows 11 represents a new era in the world of operating systems. As the latest version of Microsoft's Windows OS, Windows 11 comes with visual changes and under-the-hood improvements that aim to provide a more modern, secure, and user-friendly computing experience. While retaining the familiar Windows interface, Windows 11 introduces new features and enhancements that may require some adaptation from previous Windows users.

For over three decades, Windows has been the dominant operating system for the vast majority of computing devices globally. As technology has evolved, Microsoft has consistently released new iterations of Windows to match the capabilities of emerging hardware and the needs of users. Windows 11 represents the first major visual redesign since Windows 8. It refines the classic Windows experience with a streamlined interface centered around simplifying user workflows. Significant under-the-hood architecture changes also aim to provide better performance and security compared to previous versions.

Visually, Windows 11 features a clean, modern design with rounded corners, new icons, pastel colors, and an overall minimalist aesthetic. The iconic Start menu has been moved to the center of the taskbar at the bottom of the screen by default. Live preview thumbnails make finding open windows easier, while new sounds and animations modernize the experience. The overall effect is a calmer, more organized interface designed to help users focus on their work.

Several new features aim to boost productivity. Snap layouts allow users to arrange multiple windows in customized configurations for multitasking. Virtual desktops enable easier workspace organization. Focus sessions minimize distractions by pausing notifications. Integrations with Microsoft Teams and other apps streamline communication and collaboration. Tablet and touch enhancements create a more natural experience on 2-in-1 devices.

Performance and security also see notable improvements. Windows 11 can recover from start-up issues quickly via a new diagnostic and recovery environment. Hardware requirements aim to ensure devices run smoothly. The adoption of the highly secure Pluton architecture guards against emerging cyberthreats. The OS connects directly to the Microsoft Store for safer app downloads. Overall, Windows 11 provides a more optimized and protected environment.

For new and intermediate users, upgrading offers many advantages. The refreshed interface introduces welcome visual appeal while retaining familiar elements like the taskbar and Start menu. Smooth multi-tasking, a customizable desktop, and built-in security provide tangible quality-of-life improvements. Connectivity across the Windows ecosystem enables seamless transitions between different devices. As Microsoft supports Windows 11 far into the future, opting for their latest OS ensures continued compatibility with new software and innovations.

Transitioning to Windows 11 does require some degree of learning, especially for those comfortable with previous versions. The relocated Start menu, system tray, taskbar, and other elements may prove disorienting initially. Some settings menus have moved or been renamed. Certain workflows and shortcuts no longer apply. Older computers may encounter compatibility issues during upgrade. As with any major change, adjusting to a new digital landscape takes time, effort, and patience. But the long-term benefits make the investment worthwhile.

This book serves as a comprehensive guide to help seniors fully embrace Windows 11 as their operating system of choice. Step-by-step instructions make the upgrade process smooth and unintimidating. Clear explanations outline the new interface elements and core capabilities of Windows 11 using senior-friendly language. Tutorials provide the essential computer skills seniors need to complete day-to-day tasks confidently. Thoughtful insights address seniors' unique needs and concerns. By the end of this journey, Windows 11 will feel familiar, intuitive, and filled with potential. The road ahead may seem uncertain at first, but with this book as a companion, the path becomes clear. Windows 11 awaits.

The Differences Between Windows 11 and Previous Versions

For longtime Windows users, the release of Windows 11 in 2021 marked a major update to the familiar Windows operating system. While the upgrade offers visual changes and new features, the underlying functionality remains largely the same. This provides a balance of new capabilities without an overly steep learning curve for those transitioning from Windows 10 or earlier versions.

Fresh New Design

Perhaps the most immediately noticeable change is Windows 11's fresh aesthetic. Microsoft overhauled the design language to be cleaner, more modern, and more visually appealing.

Some of the most prominent design upgrades include rounded corners on windows and menus, pastel backgrounds, softer icon designs, and the centralized Start menu and taskbar. The subtle transparency effects give a sense of depth while maintaining readability.

Overall, the new look aims to improve content focus without excessive visual clutter. It aligns with Microsoft's Fluent Design System, which emphasizes lighting, depth, motion, materiality, and scale. This creates a familiar yet more refined user experience.

Redesigned Start Menu

The Start menu sees some of the biggest changes in Windows 11. It now appears in the center of the taskbar by default, rather than the traditional left corner.

Microsoft optimized this for touchscreen devices. However, you can easily move the Start menu back to the left side if you prefer.

Within the Start menu, you'll notice a simplified layout. Live tiles are gone in favor of a clean list of pinned apps and recommendations powered by AI. Search is more tightly integrated.

There are also customizable Administrator and User account options. Overall, the reimagined Start menu focuses on simplicity and personalization.

Enhanced Taskbar

The taskbar also enjoys several upgrades. Icons are centered for consistency with the Start button. You can ungroup apps to separate their buttons.

Right click the taskbar to toggle new menu options like Taskbar settings and Task Manager. Hover over application icons to preview their open windows. Swipe to easily switch desktops.

While fundamental taskbar functionality remains the same, these changes enhance usability. Familiar tools become quicker and more convenient.

Updated Settings App

Windows Settings sees a major overhaul, which replaces the old Control Panel on many devices. Settings encompasses all your system preferences in a streamlined, user-friendly interface.

It provides wider search capabilities, attractive visual design, and intuitive organization. Settings surfaces personalized recommendations, interactive tutorials, and detailed explanations.

Key categories like Network & Internet, Personalization, Apps, Accounts, and Time & Language are easier to navigate. While Control Panel still exists, Settings will likely become your go-to for system adjustments.

Stronger Default Security

Windows 11 ushers in stronger default device security configurations. This provides enhanced protection against modern cyber threats without burdening you with complex settings.

Secure Boot prevents unauthorized programs from loading during boot. Encryption guards data from physical access attacks. Default firewall and antimalware tools add monitoring. Strengthened identity protection reduces password threats.

These measures harden your device against breaches, malware, and exploitation. With comprehensive security built-in, Windows 11 enables you to operate safely by default.

Refreshed Bundled Apps

Windows 11 introduces refreshed native apps like Mail, Calendar, Photos, Weather, and Media Player. These present a more streamlined design using WinUI and web technologies.

Performance sees optimization as well. The apps integrate tightly with Windows 11 through features like widgets and live previews. They provide a smoother experience than previous iterations.

While Microsoft Edge, Paint, Notepad, and other apps remain largely similar, the updates bring welcome improvements across the board. You can be productive right out of the box.

In summary, while Windows 11 retains the familiar Windows environment, the update introduces refinements across the board. Visually, it's a more polished OS. UI interactions feel snappier and more intuitive through design upgrades. Default security takes a big step forward as well.

For longtime Windows fans, Windows 11 balances new capabilities like Teams integration, Android app support, and AI recommendations with classic functionality. The learning curve is gentle yet rewarding.

Upgrading lets you maintain the comfort of past Windows versions you know and love while enjoying modem benefits. With thoughtful enhancements, Windows 11 feels like the natural evolution of Microsoft's defining OS.

Understanding the Windows 11 Interface

Transitioning to a new operating system often means needing to get your bearings in a new digital landscape. While Windows 11 retains the familiar Windows environment, some key changes to the interface introduce new ways of interacting and navigating the OS. Taking time to understand the layout, features, and functions of the Windows 11 interface will help ensure you can find what you need quickly and work efficiently.

At the heart of the Windows 11 interface is the Start menu and the taskbar running along the bottom of the screen. The Start menu, indicated by the Windows icon in the bottom left, is your launch pad into the apps, programs, files, and settings of Windows 11. Click it to open a menu providing quick access to frequently used apps and key system functions. The centered taskbar contains app icons for open programs, the search bar, system tray icons for things like volume control and network status, the date and time, and buttons to view open windows and switch between virtual desktops. Familiarizing yourself with the layout and capabilities of these two bars is crucial.

The desktop area displays open windows and acts as a centralized workspace. You can access your files and folders here through File Explorer, visualize documents, browse the web, and more. Right click anywhere on the desktop to access customization options for changing wallpapers, organizing layouts, and managing accessibility settings. Getting comfortable navigating between open windows via clicking, key commands, and touch gestures expands your efficiency.

Within most programs and apps, you will find three common buttons in the upper right corner: minimize, maximize, and close. Minimize shrinks a window down into just its icon on the taskbar for later access. Maximize enlarges a window to take up the full screen. Close shuts down the open window. Mastering these core functions allows smooth transitions between tasks.

One of the handiest tools for quickly accessing apps and files is the Start menu search bar. Found at the bottom of the Start menu, simply start typing to find anything on your system almost instantly. Search is one of the quickest ways to launch apps and locate documents rather than browsing through menus.

For additional settings and administrative functions, click the System icon in the Start menu. This opens the Settings app, which contains customizable options for personalizing, updating, securing, and troubleshooting your device. Things like display resolution, user accounts permissions, VPN connections, recovery options, and hardware settings reside here.

While visually streamlined, Windows 11 offers many options for customizing your workflow through the taskbar context menu. Right click the taskbar and select "Taskbar Settings" to tweak taskbar alignment and sizing, notification behavior, which icons appear, and more to best suit your needs. Don't be afraid to tailor things to optimize your experience.

The Action Center, accessed by clicking its icon on the taskbar, serves as your command center for notifications. Things like new emails, calendar events, app alerts, and more appear in the Action Center for quick access. You can customize notifications and turn off distractions here. Think of it like a digital assistant keeping you informed.

These core Windows 11 interface components aim to create a responsive, flexible, and user-friendly environment. While learning new digital landscapes takes patience and practice, Microsoft designed Windows 11 to feel intuitive. With some guided exploration and experimentation, its functionality becomes clear.

The Advantages of Upgrading to Windows 11

With its fresh visual design and array of new capabilities, Windows 11 marks an exciting evolution for Microsoft's leading operating system. Upgrading from Windows 10 or earlier versions brings meaningful benefits that enhance your computing experience.

Improved UI Design

As discussed in the previous chapter, Windows 11 introduces a cleaner, more modern UI design. Rounded corners, transparency effects, pastel colors, and extra padding between elements help reduce visual clutter.

This refined aesthetic makes the OS more pleasant and comfortable to look at while improving content focus. The centered Start menu and taskbar also provide better ergonomics for devices with touchscreens. Overall, Windows 11's user interface feels more organic and unified.

Enhanced Gaming Features

Gaming demonstrates noticeable improvements in Windows 11. The new OS optimizes overall performance and latency for a competitive edge.

Auto HDR provides richer color and contrast by automatically enabling high dynamic range for supported games. DirectStorage loads assets faster by reducing CPU overhead. An integrated Xbox app offers perks like Game Pass.

Windows 11 also introduces DirectX 12 Ultimate for immersive graphics at high frame rates. For gaming, the upgrade brings demonstrable performance and visual perks.

Improved Multitasking

More advanced multitasking capabilities also come built-in with Windows 11. Snap layouts automatically arrange apps into efficient configurations for productivity.

Snap groups keep collections of apps open to swap between multiple tasks. New keyboard shortcuts amplify multitasking speed. Virtual desktops help keep your spaces organized.

Windows 11 multitasking enhancements empower users to operate more efficiently. You can get more done in less time.

Access Android Apps

One truly unique addition is Android app support on Windows 11 devices. The new Amazon Appstore enables installing popular mobile apps and games.

This brings over half a million Android apps into Windows for the first time. You can now enjoy apps like Kindle, Audible, Subway Surfers, and Khan Academy on your PC. Seamless integration with Intel Bridge technology ensures performance.

Accessing this vast library of Android software vastly expands possibilities for entertainment and productivity. It's a game changer for Windows.

AI-Powered Features

Windows 11 infuses artificial intelligence across the OS to create smarter, more personalized experiences. This is most visible with widgets on the personalized Start menu.

Widgets surfaces news, weather, sports highlights, calendar events, and other updates catered specifically to you. The content refreshes constantly to deliver glanceable information when you need it.

Other AI examples include in-call captions for live transcriptions and Focus Sessions to mitigate distractions. Windows 11 uses AI to get to know you and serve you better.

Improved Default Security

As mentioned earlier, Windows 11 provides the most robust default device security in Windows history. This means your device becomes instantly more secure upon upgrading, without any settings changes required.

Upgraded protections like Secure Boot, encryption, and Microsoft Defender Antivirus will keep you much safer against modern cyber threats. Improving security is reason enough for many users to upgrade.

Ongoing Innovation

The benefits highlighted represent just a sample of Windows 11 capabilities. Microsoft plans to continue introducing new features and enhancements through regular OS updates.

This ongoing innovation ensures Windows 11 will only become more useful and more polished over time. Upgrading now allows you to enjoy the latest features as they become available.

Setting Expectations: What this Book Covers

Embarking on learning a new operating system can feel daunting. With so many features and functions to take in, it's natural to wonder: What exactly will this book cover? By setting clear expectations upfront, we can map out the path ahead so you can approach Windows 11 with confidence. This introductory chapter aims to broadly outline the core concepts, skills, and resources this book will equip you with on your journey towards Windows 11 mastery.

First and foremost, this book focuses on the essentials - the key tasks and tools Windows 11 provides to help you work, browse, communicate, and get things done digitally. Step-by-step guidance will cover must-know functions like installing apps, organizing files, customizing settings, navigating the web, emailing, accessing media content, and more.

Explanations use straightforward language and examples tailored for beginners. The goal is to get you up and running with the capabilities you'll actually use daily.

While covering the basics, this book also dives deeper into helping you gain true comfort and independence using your device. Tips, tricks, and best practices provide insider know-how to boost efficiency and understanding. Troubleshooting advice handles common problems if they arise. Discussions highlight customization options, accessibility features, security considerations, and other senior-specific needs. The insights interwoven throughout aim to anticipate your questions and concerns.

In terms of technical ground covered, you can expect the following core Windows 11 topics explained:

- Installing and getting started with Windows 11
- Navigating the desktop, Start menu, and system settings
- Working with apps, programs, files and folders
- Using Microsoft Edge for web browsing
- Setting up email and understanding online communication methods
- Personalizing your PC, adjusting accessibility settings as needed
- Maintaining performance, updates, backups, and security
- Leveraging Windows 11 tips and tricks for seniors

While thoroughly covering Windows 11 itself, this book also briefly introduces integrating with Microsoft 365, including apps like Word, Excel, Outlook, OneDrive, and more. Supplementing the OS with tools for communication, productivity, and organization expands what you can achieve.

However, no single book can cover everything. The digital world expands every day. So consider this guide a starting point. As your skills and interests grow, many resources exist to build upon these foundations at your own pace. The doors that Windows 11 opens are endless.

In terms of teaching approach, expect straightforward language, step-by-step guidance, visual references, and hands-on examples that clearly illustrate concepts. You won't just read about features—you'll actively practice and apply what you learn through activities. Retention comes by doing. Chapters intentionally build upon each other for gradual mastery. Additionally, don't hesitate to revisit chapters if needed to reinforce your knowledge.

This book will also emphasize cultivating the confidence needed to explore Windows 11 independently over time and troubleshoot issues as they arise. Digital literacy takes patience, persistence, and practice. Mistakes will happen as part of the learning curve. What matters is having the resilience to problem solve solutions. As long as you retain curiosity and determination, you will succeed.

By the final page, the once foreign elements of Windows 11 will feel familiar and intuitive. Working digitally will transition from intimidating to empowering. Consider this book a knowledgeable guide walking beside you through unfamiliar terrain, pointing out hazards to avoid and sights not to miss. Together the path ahead becomes clearer, one step at a time.

The digital world won't always feel comfortable or easy to navigate at first. But with the right insights and support, Windows 11 can open up new possibilities that enhance how you live, work, and connect in our technology-driven society. Let the journey begin!

CHAPTER 1

GETTING STARTED WITH WINDOWS 11

Installing or Upgrading to Windows 11

Installing Windows 11 on a new PC or upgrading from an older Windows version represents the first step in your Windows 11 journey. Thankfully, Microsoft designed the process to be simple and intuitive for both clean installs and upgrades.

Clean Install on a New Computer

If you purchase a new Windows 11 computer, chances are the OS will come pre-installed. However, you may need to go through the initial device setup steps before using it.

The setup wizard will guide you through choosing your region and language, connecting to the internet, accepting Microsoft's terms of service, personalizing Windows with your account details, and configuring basic device settings like privacy options.

Follow the on-screen instructions until you reach the Windows 11 desktop. The process is designed for beginners and should only take about 10-15 minutes. Then you can start enjoying your new computer right away!

Upgrading from an Earlier Version of Windows

For existing machines running Windows 10, 8, or 7, you will need to manually perform the upgrade process. The good news is that it is remarkably straightforward.

Microsoft recommends checking your system meets the minimum hardware requirements prior to upgrading. This includes things like processor generation, RAM amount, storage space and TPM 2.0 support.

The Windows 11 upgrade is free for valid Windows 10 licenses. To get started, open Windows Update in your current OS version. Click "Check for updates" and install any available updates first.

Then the Windows 11 upgrade should appear for download. Click to install it like any other update. Your system will restart several times during the process. Follow the prompts until you reach the new Windows 11 desktop.

Clean Installing Windows 11

If you wish to do a fresh Windows 11 installation without upgrading from an existing OS, you can create installation media and boot from it.

You will need a blank 8GB+ USB drive and a Windows 11 ISO image, available for free from Microsoft. Download the Media Creation Tool to automatically configure the drive.

Boot your target installation PC from the USB drive. Follow the step-by-step setup wizard to choose language, partition hard drives as desired, configure settings, and create user accounts.

Once complete, you will boot directly into your fresh Windows 11 OS, ready for you to install programs and customize. This approach works great for new PC builds or replacing old OS versions.

Tips for a Smooth Installation

Here are some tips to ensure your Windows 11 installation or upgrade goes smoothly:

- Back up important data in case anything goes wrong during installation.
- Close all programs and save your work before starting the upgrade.
- Keep your computer plugged into a power source during installation to avoid interruptions.
- Connect to the internet via Ethernet if possible for fastest speeds.
- Disable antivirus software temporarily to prevent potential conflicts.
- Read all prompts carefully and wait for processes to complete before advancing.
- Restart when prompted to ensure changes fully apply.

Following these best practices will help set you up for a quick, painless installation experience. Take things slowly and let the process work without interrupting. Within an hour or two, you should be greeted by your new Windows 11 environment, ready for customization.

Enjoy the Benefits

As discussed in the previous chapter, Windows 11 offers many excellent benefits over previous Windows generations. Upgrading or installing provides access to all of these new capabilities that can streamline your computing experience.

With a refreshed design, expanded features, and ongoing updates, Windows 11 is absolutely worth the effort to install on your devices. The process is designed for simplicity and ease. In no time at all, you can have the latest Windows OS enhancing both productivity and entertainment.

Navigating the Windows 11 Desktop

Welcome to your Windows 11 desktop - this space will serve as your central hub for productivity and digital tasks. Learning to navigate this digital workspace confidently is crucial for success.

The desktop itself refers to the background area on your screen where you can access apps and programs, view and arrange open windows, store file shortcuts and generally manage your workflow. Customizing this space to suit your needs makes working here more efficient. Right click the desktop background and select "Personalize" to change wallpaper images, colors, and themes to your taste.

A key component of the desktop is the taskbar running across the bottom. This contains the Start menu button, search bar, app icons for open programs, system tray for things like volume control and network status, the time/date display, virtual desktop switching buttons and a view of all open windows. Mastering navigation via the taskbar is essential.

The Start menu, opened by clicking the Windows icon in the bottom left, contains quick access shortcuts to frequently used apps, important system functions like power options, user profiles, settings and file exploration. Memorize the layout here since you will be accessing it constantly.

The search bar built into the taskbar lets you instantly find apps, documents, system tools and more by just typing keywords rather than browsing through menus. Search is one of the quickest ways to access things on your PC.

Minimizing windows shrinks them down to just their icon on the taskbar for easy access later. Maximizing enlarges windows to fill the full screen for focused work. Close fully shuts down open windows when done. Master these three buttons for efficient window switching.

Keyboard shortcuts like Alt + Tab allow rapid switching between open windows. Alt + F4 closes the active window. The Windows key opens the Start menu. Learning hotkeys will greatly boost productivity.

Touch gestures like swiping in from the sides or corners are an intuitive way to access search, Task View, widgets and notifications. Enable touch in Settings if using a 2-in-1 device.

Right clicking the taskbar opens customization options like rearranging icons, changing sizing, hiding labels and more. Tailor things to best suit your workflow style.

The system tray area containing the time, WiFi, volume and other icons can be expanded by clicking the up arrow. This reveals hidden icons and quick access to their settings.

Virtual desktops are like having multiple separate workspaces you can switch between instantly. Create and organize different desktops for each aspect of your digital life.

File Explorer, accessed via the taskbar or Start menu, contains your full library of files, folders and downloads. Stay organized here to easily find documents. Pin important folders like Documents or Pictures for quick access.

The desktop may seem busy at first, but following visual cues and practicing navigation between elements builds muscle memory quickly. Customize your workspace to match how you prefer to work. With guided exploration, this digital landscape will soon feel comfortable and intuitive. Patiently learning the fundamentals prepares you for efficient mastery.

Understanding Basic Windows 11 Terminology

As you learn to navigate Windows 11, you will encounter new terms and concepts. Understanding this basic Windows vocabulary is essential for fully grasping how to use your computer.

The Desktop

The desktop refers to the main workspace screen you see after logging into Windows. It provides access to your files, apps, taskbar, Start menu, and other program windows.

You can customize the desktop background image and arrange shortcuts for quick access. It represents the central hub for launching programs and managing content.

Icons

Icons are small graphical images that represent different files, folders, drives, apps, system functions, and more in Windows.

For example, the Recycle Bin is represented by an icon of a wastebasket. Icons allow you to quickly identify items visually. You can double click icons to open associated programs or files.

Taskbar

The taskbar is the bar spanning the bottom of the Windows desktop. It contains icons for open apps, the Start button, system tray, and more.

You can launch tasks, switch between programs, adjust volume, view the time, and access other controls quickly using the taskbar without having to open menus. It remains visible on top of other windows.

Start Menu

Accessible via the Start button in the bottom left corner, the Start menu provides quick access to installed apps, key system functions like power options, user accounts, settings, and search.

Click the Start button or press the Windows key to open the menu. Within it, find apps, shut down your PC, or customize Windows settings.

File Explorer

File Explorer provides the interface for browsing, managing, and manipulating files and folders on your Windows device and connected storage drives.

Within File Explorer, you can copy, move, rename, delete, zip, and otherwise organize your documents, media, downloads, and other files.

System Tray

The system tray occupies the rightmost section of the taskbar. It contains icons representing actively running apps and background processes like security tools and printers.

Right click the system tray icons to control features like Wi-Fi, volume, notifications, touch pad settings, and more without having to open each full app.

Settings

Settings provides access to customize all aspects of Windows 11 through an attractive, organized interface. Open Settings via the Start menu to configure devices, apps, personalization, accounts, updates, privacy and more.

It replaces the outdated Control Panel as the primary location for accessing and adjusting your system preferences and options.

Live Tiles

Live tiles are customizable blocks that can display dynamically updated information and app content on the Start menu. For example, the Weather tile updates to show current conditions.

While very useful, live tiles are removed in Windows 11. The new Start menu focuses solely on pinned apps and recommended content powered by AI.

Desktop Shortcuts

You can create desktop shortcuts for quick access to frequently used files, folders, apps, websites and other items. Shortcuts appear as icons on your desktop.

Simply right-click an item and select "Create shortcut" or drag and drop the item to your desktop. Double click shortcuts to quickly open the associated app or file.

Action Center

The Action Center appears when you click its icon in the taskbar system tray. It provides notifications like new messages and alerts from apps and settings shortcuts like Wi-Fi controls.

Access missed notifications and configure notification settings quickly through the Action Center without having to open each related app individually.

Apps and Programs

Apps and programs refer to the software installed on your Windows device. Examples include the Microsoft Edge browser, Mail and Calendar apps, Excel and other Office programs, games, utilities and more.

Apps are typically small, lightweight modern applications while programs can reference more robust desktop software. Apps are accessed via the Start menu while programs appear in the overall apps list.

Processes

Processes refer to all the apps, programs, services, background tasks, and other computing operations happening on your PC at any given time. You can view these active processes in the Task Manager.

Some processes run all the time, like security services. Others activate temporarily as needed. Ending unnecessary processes can improve system performance.

Windows Store

The Windows Store is the marketplace built into Windows for browsing, downloading, and installing apps, games, and software. Open the Store app to search among thousands of offerings, both free and paid.

Downloaded apps will appear in your Start menu for quick access. The Store lets you easily expand the capabilities of your Windows device.

With these key Windows terms defined, you have the basic vocabulary needed to understand instructions for common tasks. Refer back to this glossary anytime you need a quick refresher on core Windows concepts.

Adjusting Basic System Settings

One of the first steps to personalizing your Windows 11 experience is adjusting basic system settings to your preferences. While default settings aim to provide a reasonable configuration, customizing options for things like display, audio, power management, and device permissions allows you to tailor your PC to best suit your needs.

Display settings have a significant impact on visual comfort and accessibility. Options like brightness, color contrast, scaling text/apps to size, and orientation can help optimize your display for readability and ease of use. Navigate to Settings > System > Display to configure your preferences. If dealing with vision limitations, enabling magnification or recommended scaling eases reading strain.

Audio settings determine sound levels for system notifications, media playback, and other instances. Balancing levels for clear audibility in different contexts improves general user experience. Review speaker and microphone configurations in Settings > System > Sound to avoid disruptive volumes. Enable mono audio if dealing with hearing limitations on one side.

Power and sleep settings control when your device enters low power or locked modes to save energy. Adjusting timeouts for screen and system sleep based on your usage habits prevents lockouts from inactivity while also optimizing battery life. Review options under Settings > System > Power & Battery.

Device security begins with requiring sign-in credentials like passwords, PINs, or biometric scans to unlock your PC. Under Settings > Accounts, enforce the authentication methods you prefer to securely access your system. Leverage Windows Hello facial recognition for a seamless sign-in experience if your device supports it.

Keyboard settings allow you to customize shortcuts, swipe actions, text prediction, spelling corrections and typing sounds to streamline input methods. Navigate to Settings > Devices > Typing to tailor behaviors to your preferences. Enabling key repeat rates can assist those with mobility limitations.

Accessibility settings open up customization options to assist users with sensory, mobility or learning limitations. Enablingvisibility enhancements, audio accommodations, input modifications and other assists under Settings > Accessibility expands usability. Don't hesitate to review the possibilities here.

Privacy settings determine permissions for device usage data, location tracking, diagnostic data sharing and other behaviors that involve your personal information. Control what apps and services can access under Settings > Privacy to better safeguard your privacy. Limit data collection.

Region and language settings allow you to configure your geographic location, date/time formats, currency symbols and keyboard layouts to your locale and culture. Make adjustments under Settings > Time & Language for an optimal experience. Add secondary languages as needed.

Ease of access settings make Windows 11 more usable for those managing limitations in vision, hearing, dexterity and cognition. Enabling read aloud, focus filtering, text resizing, color inversion and other assists under Settings > Accessibility removes barriers users may face.

While navigating system settings may seem complex at first, tweaking preferences for your requirements and comfort level is essential and manageable with practice. Like configuring the perfect office chair, take time to adjust the fit and functions of Windows 11 to your needs. The system will conform nicely to your work style with thoughtful personalization. Then you can focus on your goals, not the setup.

Setting Up User Accounts

One of the first things you will do after installing Windows 11 is to configure your user account. Your user account stores your settings, files, and preferences to provide a personalized Windows experience.

Understanding User Accounts

Windows supports several account types for signing into your device. The main options include:

Administrator Account - Has full control over the system, users, and security. Can install programs, access files, create other accounts. Requires password at login. Ideal for the primary user.

Standard User Account - Limited access for basic daily use. Cannot alter security or other user accounts/settings. Simpler to use and more secure. Good for kids or guests.

Microsoft Account - Links your PC to your personal Microsoft ID to sync settings across devices. Enables access to Microsoft services like OneDrive, Skype, Mail/Calendar, Xbox gaming, and more. Convenient but less private.

Local Account - Standalone account existing only on the local PC. No synchronization across devices. Provides more privacy but less connectivity.

Different account types suit different needs. Administrator accounts offer full control while Standard ones limit access. Microsoft accounts enable synchronization while Local ones prioritize privacy.

Creating Your Administrator Account

During initial Windows setup, you will be prompted to create your Administrator account. This will be the primary account used to manage the device and install programs.

Choose a strong, secure password. Your full name can be used for the account name. Provide your details to enable personalized features. Enable Administrator privileges for this account to have full access to the system.

Once created, this account will be used to sign into Windows by default. It can be used to create any additional necessary accounts for family and friends.

Adding Standard and Child Accounts

For additional household members using your Windows 11 PC, create separate Standard user accounts for each person. This allows personalized space for files, settings, and privacy.

Open Settings > Accounts > Family & Other Users to add accounts. Click "Add account" then choose account type. Enter the desired name and password. Set child accounts to automatically sign out after designated limits.

Standard accounts prevent changing device-wide settings. Restrictions can be enacted like disabling Store purchases or limiting app usage as needed per account.

Managing Microsoft Accounts

Linking your PC to a Microsoft account enables syncing settings, history, and preferences across devices logged into the same account. It also provides access to Microsoft ecosystem features.

During Windows setup, you can choose to create or link a new or existing Microsoft account like an Outlook.com email address. You can also convert a local account later in Settings.

While convenient, Microsoft accounts do result in less privacy. Weigh the benefits against potential privacy risks for your needs.

In summary, properly configuring user accounts is vital for an organized, secure Windows experience tailored to each individual person using your device. Set up the account types that make the most sense for convenience, control, and privacy.

CHAPTER 2

MASTERING THE CORE FEATURES

The Start Menu and Taskbar

The Start menu and taskbar are central command centers that provide quick access to apps, files, settings and system functions in Windows 11. Mastering navigation and capabilities of these primary interface elements is fundamental for effectively managing your PC.

Housed in the bottom left, the Start menu is the launch pad to access everything Windows offers. The first section provides pinned tiles for frequently used apps and recommended files. Click All apps to browse the full app list alphabetically. Recently added and most used apps also display here for convenience. Account settings, power options, and key system tools reside on the left. Search, pinned app tiles, documents and system functions are just a click away.

Right click the Start button to reveal useful options like Device Manager for managing connected devices, Event Viewer for system health details, Task Manager for resource monitoring and a command prompt for technical users. Explorer, Settings and Power shortcuts provide quick access as well.

The Start menu search bar allows finding apps, documents and system tools in seconds just by typing keywords. Search is one of the fastest ways to access things compared to browsing through menus. Pin frequently used results like Control Panel to save clicks.

Scroll down the Start menu to reveal customizable Quick Settings toggles for convenient access to settings like Wi-Fi, Bluetooth, Focus Mode and more. Add or remove desired toggles here. Also customize the bottom app pins for your most used items.

The taskbar runs horizontally across the bottom and contains the Start menu button, centered Search bar, app icons for open programs, notification and system tray icons on the right and a timeline preview of open windows on the left. Master taskbar navigation for easy workflow.

Minimizing app windows condenses them down to just their icon on the taskbar for multitasking ease. Right click the icon for a menu of recent files and app controls. Maximize windows with the middle expand icon for full screen focus. Close fully when finished.

The system tray containing the clock, network, volume, etc icons can be expanded by selecting the ^ arrow. This reveals hidden icons and quick access to their settings. Customize visible icons via Taskbar Settings.

Preview thumbnails make switching between open windows easy. Hover over an app icon on the taskbar to see a live preview of the window. Click to switch to it instantly. Keyboard shortcut Alt + Tab cycles between open apps.

Right click the taskbar itself to access options for rearrange icons, tweak toolbars, enable command prompt access and more. Customizing the taskbar boosts speed and convenience.

Overall, harnessing the capabilities of the Start menu and taskbar allows smooth navigation and efficient workflow in Windows 11. Dedicate time upfront to memorizing their functions, customizing to your needs, and building navigation muscle memory. Before long, your digital landscape will feel like home.

Working with Apps and Programs

One of the first things you'll want to do in Windows 11 is install apps and programs to expand what your device can do. The good news is that Windows makes it very simple to get the software you need.

Finding Apps and Programs

The easiest way to find apps is through the Microsoft Store app pre-installed on Windows 11. Open the Store app from the Start menu to browse and search among thousands of free and paid apps sorted by category.

You can also find apps online from developer websites. Be sure to stick to reputable sites like the developer's official page to avoid malware. Check reviews and ratings before downloading.

Many programs like web browsers and Office suites can just be searched online. Download directly from the developer site. Pay close attention to the download type and follow prompts to install correctly.

Installing Apps and Programs

Installing apps from the Microsoft Store just requires clicking the "Get" button, then "Install." The app will download and install automatically, adding a shortcut to your Start menu.

For programs, begin the installation process with the downloaded installer file. Follow the prompts to customize options, accept license terms, select install location, and other steps. Wait for the install to fully complete.

You may need to restart your computer after some installs. Don't hesitate to contact the developer if you encounter issues.

Opening Apps and Programs

To open apps, click their icon on the Start menu or taskbar. You can also search for apps via the search bar and click to launch them.

For desktop programs, look for their shortcut icon on the Start menu or search for them. Some add shortcuts to the taskbar for quick access. Left click the app or shortcut icon to open it.

You can also open the File Explorer, click This PC > Local Disk C: > Program Files to find installed program executables you can double click to launch.

Switching Between Apps and Programs

To switch between open apps and programs, click their icon on the taskbar or press Alt + Tab to cycle through them. Shift + Tab cycles backwards.

Hover over the app icon on the taskbar to preview the window. Right click the icon for options like closing the app, disconnecting projectors or Bluetooth devices linked to that app session.

You can move app windows by dragging and dropping the title bar at the top. Resize by dragging edges or corners. Minimize, maximize, or exit from the top right corner buttons.

Organizing Apps

To better organize your Start menu apps, right click and choose Uninstall or Unpin less frequently used ones. Pin favored apps for priority placement.

Right click the taskbar to enable "Combine taskbar buttons" to group multiple windows of the same app into one taskbar button to reduce clutter. Rename and rearrange pinned apps as desired.

Use task view or create multiple virtual desktops to group apps by function. For example, keep entertainment apps together separate from work productivity ones to stay focused.

With practice, you'll get comfortable finding, launching, using, and organizing your Windows apps for an optimized workflow. Let us know if you need any help getting specific apps installed and set up.

Using the File Explorer

Effectively organizing, locating and managing your files and folders is essential to productivity and reducing digital clutter. The File Explorer in Windows 11 allows intuitive control over your digital documents and libraries across local storage and connected devices. Learning key features for browsing, search, organization and transfer will amplify your capability and efficiency.

Access the File Explorer via the folder icon on the taskbar or through the Start menu. The left pane displays frequent folders, OneDrive access, This PC partitioning and external devices. Click folders to view their contents in the right pane. Breadcrumb navigation at the top traces your folder path. Master orienting yourself here.

Libraries contain collected content from local and cloud sources. Documents, Pictures, Music and Video libraries consolidate files saved across devices for unified access. Right click a library to add additional folders for consolidation. Prioritize keeping libraries organized.

Select View > Change view modes to toggle layouts between extra large icons, detailed lists, compact lists and more. Toggle Show/hide > Navigation pane to expand the folder tree as needed. Custom views amplify usability.

Search box at the top right filters folders and file contents as you type. Include kind:videos, Excel spreadsheets, PowerPoint presentations etc to refine results by type. Search is the fastest navigation method.

Select multiple files and right click for operations like copy, cut, rename, delete, share and print. Master these selections for efficient document management. Ctrl and Shift keys allow adjusting multiple selections.

Pin key folders like Documents or Downloads to Quick Access in the left pane for one click access. Drag and drop files between folders and drives to copy instead of cutting. **Streamline your workflows.**

Sort folder contents by selecting column headers like Name, Date modified, Type etc. Toggle ascending and descending order for organized views. Right click columns to add customizable data points.

Options tab provides useful configuration like showing file extensions, auto-hiding navigation pane, launching File Explorer to This PC by default and more. Set your preferences.

Ribbon menu contains convenient tools like moving files to compressed zip folders, syncing to cloud services, proper file deletion and advanced searching tools. Explore its possibilities.

Overall, embracing File Explorer allows proactive control over your storage ecosystem. Develop digital housekeeping habits like routine organization, consolidation and cleaning to maintain order. Let File Explorer become second nature through regular practical use rather than just passive storage. Keep your digital documents in shape.

Customizing the Desktop and Taskbar

One of the best things about Windows is how customizable it can be. You can tailor the look and functionality of the desktop and taskbar to perfectly match your style, workflow, and preferences.

Changing the Desktop Background

The desktop background provides the canvas for your icons and windows. Setting a wallpaper you love instantly makes Windows feel more personal.

Right click the desktop and select "Personalize" to open customization options. Click "Background" to pick from included wallpaper images, solid colors, or even make a custom slideshow. You can also right click an image file and set as background.

Enabling Dark Mode

For a dramatically different look, enable Dark mode from Colors in the customization menu. This inverts white UI elements to black for a cool, modern aesthetic. It can reduce eye strain in low light.

You can schedule Dark mode to turn on automatically at sunset or set times. Toggle it manually on the quick settings panel in Action Center. Enable on a per-app basis as well.

Showing Desktop Icons

You can choose which icons appear on the desktop for quick access and visual appeal. Right click the desktop and select "Show more options" to toggle icon visibility for This PC, Recycle Bin, drives, frequent folders, and more.

Hide icons you rarely use. Bring your most important folders and items to the forefront. Reduce clutter while keeping key content handy.

Arranging the Desktop

The desktop allows you to place shortcuts, folders, and icons anywhere for your own optimized workflow. You can neatly organize content in corners or distribute evenly.

Right click items and choose "Align icons" options like "Align to grid" to automatically tidy things up. Use your spatial memory and grouping methods to stay efficient.

Customizing Taskbar Position

You can move the Windows taskbar from the default bottom position to left, right or top edges of the screen if desired.

Unlock the taskbar, then drag and drop it into place. Lock it down again if you wish. This grants flexibility for extended displays and personal preference.

Changing Taskbar Size

Adjusting the taskbar's sizing is another great option for customization and space. Unlock the taskbar and drag a vertical edge to freely resize bigger or smaller as needed.

Try reduced height to save vertical room. Increase size to display more pinned apps or make items easier to click. Set based on your display size, usage, and preferences.

With limitless ways to tweak the desktop and taskbar, you can craft a Windows environment perfect for the way you work and live. Don't hesitate to explore and experiment to find your ideal setup. Make Windows distinctly yours.

Using the Action Center and Notifications

Staying on top of alerts and messages is key for not missing important communications or system updates. The Action Center in Windows 11 collects notifications in one place for review while also providing quick access to useful settings. Learning to leverage the capabilities of the Action Center will keep you informed, responsive and in control.

The Action Center is accessed by clicking its icon on the taskbar, which will show a number badge if notifications are waiting. The panel displays recent alerts grouped by app, providing an easy way to review notifications you may have missed. Select an alert to open the associated app or content.

Common notifications include new emails, chat messages, social media activity, calendar events, app updates ready to install, security threats detected and more. Flagged notifications persist until dismissed, while others will disappear over time when reviewed.

Quick action buttons at the bottom provide one-click access to frequently used settings like Bluetooth, Wi-Fi, screen brightness, airplane mode, focus assist and many others. Customize which actions appear here via Settings.

Under notification history, toggle filtering between showing all notifications or just those flagged as priority. Apps can be toggled on or off to filter sources. Select an app name to access detailed notification settings.

In Settings > System > Notifications, deeper preferences can be configured per app for enable/disable, notification style, badges, sounds, priority levels, lock screen privacy and more. Customize to your needs.

Focus assist options in the Action Center enable limiting notifications for set periods to avoid distractions. Toggle between priority only, alarms only or complete silence as desired. Scheduling is available.

For security alerts, options exist to isolate that PC from the network, scan for threats, open Windows Security and more. Carefully review alerts and directions provided here.

In the manage notifications section of Settings, additional global behaviors can be set like default duration before dismissal, badges on taskbar icons, notifications on lock screen and priority app selection.

Overall, embracing the Action Center allows staying effortlessly informed about communications and system events while also providing easy access to key settings. Develop a habit of regularly checking notifications to avoid missing anything important. And customize firmly for optimal control.

Using the Clipboard History and Snipping Tool

Windows includes useful utilities like clipboard history and the snipping tool to enhance productivity. Clipboard history stores multiple recent copies for easy pasting while Snip & Sketch lets you capture screenshots.

Leveraging Clipboard History

The clipboard temporarily stores text, images, and files you copy or cut from apps and websites. Windows 11 takes this a step further with clipboard history.

Clipboard history saves multiple entries over time instead of just the last copy. You can quickly paste any item from your clipboard history, providing more flexibility when transferring content between apps and documents.

To access clipboard history, press the Windows key + V keyboard shortcut. This will open a overlay displaying your recent clipboard entries as clickable thumbnails.

Alternatively, open the Action Center and expand the clipboard section at the bottom. You can click any entry to paste it into the active document or app.

You can also pin important clippings to the top for persistent access. Right click entries to pin, unpin, delete, or clear all. This clipboard history streamlines content transfers.

Capturing Screenshots with Snip & Sketch

The Snip & Sketch app provides handy screenshot capture capabilities bundled into Windows. Open it from the Start menu to start snipping.

You can click and drag to manually select any portion of the screen to copy as an image. This frees you from capturing entire screens.

Use handy shortcuts like drawing a rectangle around your desired area to auto-snap a selection. New in Windows 11, hold Shift while selecting to snap a resizable window outline for clean captures.

The app includes tools for annotating your snips with text, shapes, highlighters, and more. You can save images locally or copy to your clipboard. The streamlined interface makes capturing and sharing screenshots easy.

Setting Default Snip Hotkey

For fastest access, set a custom keyboard shortcut to open Snip & Sketch.

Open Settings and go to Accessibility > Keyboard. Under Shortcut keys, assign a shortcut to "Open snipping shortcut" and enable. Now you can start snipping anywhere instantly.

You can also still access it the original way by pressing Windows key + Shift + S. But a custom hotkey lets you capture even quicker.

Snip Options and Settings

Take advantage of options within Snip & Sketch for advanced use cases. The "Delay" tool pauses capture for a set time, allowing you to prepare the target app window first.

In Settings, enable options like opening your snips in a new app window by default for easier editing and annotations. Disable the snipping sound if desired.

You can also have your screenshots save by default to the cloud via connected services like OneDrive or your local PC rather than copying to the clipboard. Adjust as needed.

With practice, Snip & Sketch will become invaluable for quick markups, sharing important information, collaborating on projects, and countless other uses. It's one of the handiest built-in Windows 11 tools.

Toni Davison

CHAPTER 3

INTERNET AND EMAIL

Setting Up Your Internet Connection

Having access to the internet unlocks an indispensable gateway to information, entertainment, communication and more. Getting online can enrich and empower daily life across many dimensions.

The most common way to connect to the internet at home involves using a Wi-Fi router broadcasting a wireless network you can join with your PC and other devices. Start by ensuring your router is powered on and broadcasting by checking for its network name in the Wi-Fi settings. Select the router's SSID and enter the password if prompted to connect.

For the best Wi-Fi range and speeds, position your router centrally and avoid interference from objects, thick walls or distances. Connect via ethernet cable when possible for faster, more reliable performance. Upgrading to newer router hardware can also amplify speeds and coverage.

If away from home, public Wi-Fi hotspots from cafes, libraries, hotels and commercial spaces allow conveniently getting online. However, avoid accessing sensitive accounts on public networks and use a VPN app to encrypt your connection for privacy. Limit exposure.

Cellular mobile hotspots utilize your smartphone or a dedicated hotspot device to share its cellular data connection via Wi-Fi. This provides connectivity on the go when Wi-Fi is unavailable. But data usage limits can apply, so optimize for essential needs only.

For rural areas with limited broadband infrastructure, satellite internet may be an option using providers like Viasat, HughesNet and Starlink. Plans involve installing a dish antenna with open sky view. Speeds and data caps vary, but offer feasible connectivity otherwise unserved.

In Settings > Network & Internet, you can view all available nearby Wi-Fi networks, preferred networks, data usage statistics, cellular data options if supported, VPN configurations, proxy settings, network sharing preferences and more.

Troubleshoot connectivity issues by restarting your router and PC, clearing stored network settings, checking cabling, router admin settings, antenna adjustments, ISP service status and more. Run network diagnostics via Windows for automated fixes.

Patience and persistence are key in solving internet connectivity problems. Document service calls, firmware updates, observations and solutions thoroughly. Don't hesitate to contact your ISP and router manufacturer for tech support. Online resources also provide helpful tutorials.

Once stable internet access is established, settling into familiar websites and apps will make the digital world feel closer and friendlier. While connectivity brings growing pains, overcoming challenges forges self-sufficiency. And staying determined opens doors to lifelong learning and enrichment online.

Navigating the Web with Microsoft Edge

The web browser is one of the most important and often used applications on a computer. Microsoft Edge provides the default browser included with Windows 11. It combines speed, performance, stability, and built-in features to deliver a robust browsing experience.

Launching Microsoft Edge

Microsoft Edge places a shortcut icon on the taskbar during Windows 11 installation. Click this icon at any time to launch the browser.

You can also press the Windows key and type "Edge" to find and open it that way. Pin it to your Start menu to create an additional access point.

Edge will launch and open to a default home page. This is fully customizable, which we'll cover soon. From the home page, you can search or enter web addresses to visit sites and begin browsing.

Navigating Web Pages

Navigating through web pages is easy with Edge. Click links to navigate to pages on the current site. The Back and Forward arrow buttons let you move between pages in history.

To visit new websites, type the full web address into the address bar at the top and hit Enter to go there directly. Use the Refresh button to the left of the address to reload the current page.

Edge also supports intuitive touchscreen gestures like swiping left/right to go back/forward between pages and scrolling to move up and down on the current page.

Searching on the Web

To search the web, simply type keywords into the address bar or search field and press Enter. Edge will display search results powered by the Bing search engine by default.

You can open the menu by clicking the three dots at the top right to change the default search engine to Google, Yahoo, or others if desired.

For more advanced searches, use quotation marks for an exact match phrase, a dash to exclude words, or tools like site: to limit results to a specific website. The address bar doubles as a versatile search box.

Configuring Settings

Take advantage of Settings (accessed via the three dot menu) to customize Edge to your preferences. You can set default pages, change search engines, manage autofill and passwords, enable reading view, and much more.

For example, under Appearance you can enable a dark theme or adjust text sizing. Manage extensions, site permissions, languages, and other options as well. Make Edge work the way you want.

Flagging Downloads

Edge will flag downloads from less reputable sites to protect you from malware and viruses. If you try downloading an unsafe file type like an .exe from an unknown site, Edge will block the download and warn you of potential risks.

You can choose to ignore the risk and download anyways, but it's safest to avoid untrusted sources. Stick to official sites and app stores to stay secure.

Using Reading View

To minimize distractions for long articles, click the book icon to enable Reading View. This strips away menus, ads, and pictures to focus solely on the main text content.

Make the font larger for improved readability. Convert pages to a virtual ebook. Adjust colors and layout as desired. Reading View reduces clutter when you want to concentrate.

Overall, Edge provides a robust set of features for safe, customizable browsing. With practice navigating web pages, settings, and search, it will become a vital gateway to internet resources and content.

Introduction to Email and Setting up Mail

Email remains one of the foremost digital communication mediums for its convenience, versatility and ubiquity. Learning email fundamentals, setting up your preferred address, and customizing account settings optimizes managing your inbox. We'll cover everything from understanding addresses to blocking spam so your mailbox becomes a productive tool rather than a burden.

An email address follows the basic format - your chosen username followed by @ symbol and the mail provider domain (gmail.com, hotmail.com, etc). When choosing your name, opt for variations of your real name or initials for professional contexts, and fun phrases for personal use.

Leading email providers like Gmail, Outlook and Yahoo offer free sign-up with web access and apps for all devices. Choose based on storage space, customization options and whether you already use other services from that brand.

When creating your account, provide basic profile info, pick a strong password, enable two-factor authentication for added security, and agree to TOS. Write down your credentials in a safe place for reference.

The inbox view displays received emails and sorting options like date, attachments, unread status, etc. Click an email to open it. Buttons allow reply, forwarding, deletion, etc. Different folders organize content like drafts, sent items and spam.

Under settings, configure things like account name display, signatures, responses, forwarding, notifications, themes and inbox types like tabs or multiple inboxes. Customize profusely.

Top controls allow composing new emails by entering recipient addresses, adding a subject line, attaching files from your PC, and formatting text. Take care to avoid spelling and grammar errors.

Safe emailing depends on not opening unexpected attachments or links, avoiding spam replies, and being wary of phishing attempts trying to steal credentials or information. When in doubt, delete.

Use block/report spam buttons on suspicious messages so filters learn and improve over time. Check junk folder periodically for incorrectly flagged emails too. Manage ruthlessly.

For productivity, embrace email folder organization with labels, apply flags for follow-up, archive older exchanges, and leverage scheduling/reminders so messages don't get lost. Tame your inbox, don't let it tame you!

Patience and attentiveness keep inboxes hazard-free and functional. But don't become overwhelmed. Setting boundaries on response times and notifications prevents email overload. Master your mailbox with focus and care.

Best Practices for Internet Safety

The internet is an invaluable resource, but also carries inherent risks if you aren't careful. When used safely, the web can enrich your life. But things like viruses, scams, and data theft can ruin an otherwise positive experience.

Using Strong Passwords

Never underestimate the value of strong, unique passwords for every account and website. Weak reused passwords make you vulnerable to credential theft and account hijacking.

Use unpredictable passwords over 12 characters combining upper and lowercase letters, numbers, and symbols. Consider a password manager app to both generate and store secure passwords. Enable two-factor authentication when possible as well.

Keeping Software Updated

Always keep Windows, your browser, antivirus software, and other apps fully updated. Updates patch security flaws and bugs that malicious actors exploit. Turn on auto-updates where possible or periodically check manually.

Don't ignore update prompts. If an app stops getting updates, it's time to replace it. Running outdated software makes you an easy target.

Avoiding Suspicious Links

Exercise caution before clicking links in emails, messages, popups, and online ads. Rest the mouse over links to inspect their true destination.

If a shortened link hides the full URL, don't click. Telltale signs of unsafe links include misspellings, unusual domains, and unexpected messages urging you to click. When in doubt, verify links through a search first or simply avoid clicking.

Securing Public Wi-Fi

Free public Wi-Fi is insecure by nature. On public networks, use a VPN to encrypt your connection and hide your traffic. Avoid accessing sensitive accounts like banking and email.

Stick to basic browsing and turn off sharing services. For optimal security, tether your smartphone's cellular connection while out and about instead of relying on open Wi-Fi.

Using Antivirus Software

Quality antivirus software provides real-time protection by scanning downloads, flagging suspicious sites, and quarantining potential threats. Windows Security handles basics, but added protection doesn't hurt.

conduct research to choose a trustworthy premium antivirus app with high marks from independent testing labs. Schedule regular scans to catch any malware that may slip through. Proactive scanning enhances safety.

Backing Up Important Data

Ransomware and hardware failures can jeopardize your files. Plan for the worst with comprehensive backups using external drives and cloud storage. Schedule regular backups and keep drives disconnected for protection.

Encrypted cloud backup provides an extra layer of protection in case local drives are damaged, stolen, or encrypted by malware. Backups minimize potential losses in disastrous scenarios.

Securing Home Wi-Fi

For home Wi-Fi, start by changing the default router username and password. Enable WPA2 or WPA3 encryption in settings and use a strong Wi-Fi password that others wouldn't easily guess.

Disable WPS, NAT-PMP port forwarding, and Universal Plug and Play to reduce exploitation risks. Use a unique SSID without your address. Stay on top of router firmware updates as well.

Practicing General Caution

More broadly, exercise caution and critical thinking with all online activities. If something seems too good to be true, it probably is. Verify claims through reputable sources.

Understand how your data will be used before submitting forms and signing up for services. Evaluate the risks before downloading anything or disabling default security settings. Let prudence guide your online decision making.

No one is immune from internet threats, but sensible precautions greatly minimize risks. Incorporate strong passwords, updated software, secure backups, antivirus scans, Wi-Fi safety, and general discretion into your daily internet use.

Introduction to Search Engines and Online Research

The internet opens up endless information if you know where and how to search. Mastering online research via search engines and savvy browsing strategies enables self-sufficient learning and problem solving. We'll cover search engine basics, crafting effective queries, evaluating sources, and research tips to turn the internet into your personal reference library.

Search engines like Google and Bing allow locating specific websites, images, videos, news and other content through keyword queries. The engine scours the web and returns ranked results based on relevance. Google dominates with over 90% market share currently.

Query construction is key for accurate results. Identify a few distinctive keywords that narrow your focus, while avoiding general terms that yield too much. "Presidential election" is better than just "election". Enable "SafeSearch" filters to avoid explicit content.

Review search operators like quotes for exact match, minus to exclude words, site: to restrict a domain, related: for similar pages, define: for definitions and more. Leverage advanced techniques.

Scan result snippets for relevance before clicking. Avoid ads, sponsored or promotional results. Verify site credibility by presence of contact info, about pages, sources cited and non-biased tone. Cross-check data.

Image searches help visualize concepts and topics visually. Tools allow usage rights filtering and reverse image lookup to trace origins. Great for illustrations.

Video search incorporates filters like duration, date, resolution and subtitles. But exercise caution - amateur footage isn't verified. Prefer clips from news, educational sources.

Specialized directories like Wikipedia, dictionary sites, medical/gov databases have authoritative information given their managed sourcing. Explore niche tools.

Develop savvy browsing habits like never downloading anything unexpectedly, avoiding sketchy sites, verifying HTTPS secure connections, and being alert to fake login prompts. Stay safe!

Practice iterative searches by reviewing initial results, refining keywords for precision, adding filters like type:pdf for supplemental materials, and digging deeper until satisfied. Perseverance pays off in finding the perfect source.

Embrace online research skills to unlock knowledge independently right from your desktop. With the right strategy and discernment, the internet becomes the ultimate reference library. Keep your curiosity alive through constant learning!

Understanding Cookies, Pop-ups, and Ad Blockers

As you browse the web, you'll encounter terms like cookies, pop-ups, and ad blockers. Understanding these common concepts will help you manage settings, tighten security, and improve your browsing experience. We'll define each term and explain the role they play when using the internet on your Windows device.

What are Cookies?

Cookies are small text files stored by websites in your browser to identify your device and remember information that makes your experience more convenient.

For example, cookies remember form inputs, website preferences, login credentials, shopping cart contents, and more so those don't have to be reset every visit. Cookies are essential for usable website functionality.

Cookies set by the sites you directly interact with are called first-party cookies and are generally benign. However, third-party cookies placed by partners and advertisers can be used to track your activity across sites. Manage cookie settings accordingly.

How to Control Cookies

You can configure cookie settings in your browser's privacy or security options. Options vary by browser but may include:

- Block all cookies by default
- Allow cookies only from sites you directly visit
- Block third-party cookies specifically
- Clear cookies and site data on exit
- Allow exceptions for trusted sites

Adjust settings based on your privacy priorities. Just know that blocking all cookies makes many sites frustrating to use. A balanced approach allows key site functionality while enhancing privacy.

Pop-up Basics

Pop-ups are new browser windows opened in front of the current window. They can contain advertisements, newsletters sign up forms, notifications, or other content a site wants to display prominently.

Pop-ups range from mildly annoying to highly intrusive. Thankfully, modern browsers include pop-up blockers you can leverage.

Controlling Pop-ups

All major browsers include built-in pop-up blocking you can enable for a cleaner browsing experience. Chrome, Edge, and Firefox block most pop-ups by default in their latest versions.

Alternatively, install a third-party pop-up blocker as a browser extension for broader protection based on keyword blocking and other advanced criteria.

You can selectively allow pop-ups on a per-site basis if needed. But a universal block stops disruptive windows from interrupting your web surfing.

Understanding Ad Blockers

Ad blockers are browser extensions that stop advertisements from loading on pages you visit. They improve page load speeds and visual appeal by removing distractions.

Ad blockers stop third-party trackers and malicious ads that compromise privacy and security. Downsides include site revenue losses and potential content blocking errors. Evaluate tradeoffs carefully when using ad blockers.

Ad Blocking Options

All major browsers offer ad blocking extensions like uBlock Origin and AdBlock Plus. Install the extension then customize filtering rules and whitelisted sites within the plugin interface.

Alternatively, privacy-focused browsers like Brave and Firefox focus on built-in ad blocking. Enable options like tracking protection to automatically strip ads without extensions.

Understanding key web browsing concepts like cookies, pop-ups, and ads allows you to thoughtfully configure ideal defaults, extensions, and settings in Windows browsers like Edge.

CHAPTER 4

COMMUNICATING AND CONNECTING

Understanding Social Media

Social media represents a digital realm for community, entertainment and engagement - but also has risks. Learning fundamentals, setting healthy boundaries and leveraging social platforms positively can make them enriching. We'll survey the social media landscape, provide best practices and maximize the upsides while navigating the downsides.

Major social platforms like Facebook, Twitter, Instagram, YouTube, LinkedIn and Pinterest each have different focuses, from friends and family to interests and videos, professional networking or inspiration. Choose wisely based on your goals.

Handle signing up with the usual precautions - unique secure password, limit personal details shared, be skeptical of promotional offers, and read privacy policies closely regarding data collection. Your choices matter.

Finding old friends, groups for your hobbies, and celebrities to follow makes social sites engaging at first. But avoid the illusion of connections without depth. Prioritize quality over quantity of followers.

Social etiquette still applies online. Pause before posting anything you wouldn't say publicly in-person. Remember your comments reflect on you professionally and personally. Post responsibly.

Limit oversharing personal activities, contact info, home locations, family details and other avenues for potential misuse. Not everyone has good intentions. Keep social media semi-anonymous.

Routinely prune friends/followers, update privacy settings, leave groups that become toxic and disengage from harmful influences. Keep your social bubble healthy.

Enable login notifications, secure account recovery options and two-factor authentication to help safeguard your profile and data. Nothing is 100% secure, but prudent precautions help.

Be very wary of misinformation on social sites. Look for trusted sources, verified accounts and confirmation from reputable outlets. Controversy drives engagement, not truth.

Monitor time spent socializing in a balanced way. Enable usage reminders if needed. Social engagement should complement real world relationships, not replace them.

With mindfulness and moderation, social media can provide entertainment, useful connections and a sense of community. But avoid pitfalls like misinformation, unhealthy comparisons and overdependence. A little socializing goes a long way.

Setting Up and Using Skype

Skype is a popular communication platform that enables free video chatting, voice calls, messaging, and file sharing with individuals or groups. Thanks to deep integration with Windows 11, Skype is easy to set up and convenient to use on your PC.

Downloading Skype

If Skype didn't come pre-installed on your Windows 11 device, you can download it for free from the Microsoft Store. Just search for "Skype" and install the desktop app to your PC.

Skype is also available as a web app you can use within your browser without installing anything. This offers added flexibility.

Creating Your Skype Account

Once Skype is installed, you'll be prompted to create or sign into your Microsoft account. This links Skype to your existing or newly created Microsoft ID.

You can use an Outlook.com email or setup a new email and password specifically for your Microsoft account. Provide your name, birthday, and phone number during account creation.

This basic information personalizes Skype contact requests and profiles. Your Microsoft account enables syncing Skype across devices.

Configuring Your Skype Profile

Within the Skype app, click your profile picture and select "Edit profile" to customize details visible to your contacts.

You can upload a profile photo, add a mood message, share your location, and provide additional information about yourself that contacts will see.

Updating these details helps your friends and family recognize you easily on Skype. Leave anything you don't want public blank for privacy.

Finding Skype Contacts

Skype gives you multiple ways to find people you know already using the platform. Click the People tab to:

- Sync contacts from your Microsoft account or phone
- Search Skype directories by name or email
- View recent conversations
- See suggestions based on your Microsoft contacts
- Add contacts manually using their Skype ID or phone number

Connecting on Skype requires both parties to add each other, so coordinate mutually adding each other as Skype connections.

Starting Calls and Chats

Calling contacts on Skype is as easy as clicking the phone or video icon beside their profile. Call quality depends on both users' internet speeds for stability.

You can also double click a contact to open a chat window and start messaging back and forth. Share files, photos, and websites by dragging and dropping attachments right into chats.

Skype chats, calls, and voicemails are seamlessly synced across mobile and desktop. Switch between devices mid-conversation if needed.

Using Skype Features

Take advantage of Skype tools like screen sharing, call recording, live captions/translations, background blur, and schedule meeting links to enhance communication:

- Screen sharing allows displaying your screen to participants during a call for presentations or visual aid.
- Call recording can capture audio and video calls as files to reference later.
- Live captions transcribe calls in real time, while translations allow multi-language calls.
- Background blur hides messy rooms by blurring everything behind you.
- Scheduling links let you create virtual meetings and invite others via shareable links.

Customizing Settings

Take time to explore Skype settings and customize to your preferences. You can configure your mic, speakers and camera, enable automatic call answering, set status options like away when idle or invisible to hide online status, enable SMS connectivity, and more. Skype offers abundant personalization based on how you communicate.

From casual video calls with faraway friends to international business conferences, Skype facilitates connection. Set it up on your Windows PC to unleash the benefits of modern communication.

Introduction to Microsoft Teams

Microsoft Teams represents a virtual collaboration hub for group messaging, video calls, file sharing and managing remote work. Learning Teams fundamentals can maximize productivity and connection. We'll get started on key features for messaging, meetings, organization and integration.

At its core, Teams allows creating dedicated spaces for groups to communicate and coordinate. Set up teams for projects, friends, family, clubs etc. Name and customize team pages to fit their purpose.

The posts tab is the main chat window for conversations, sharing links, documents etc. @mention colleagues to draw their attention. Search chat history for references. Pins highlight important info.

Video and voice channels facilitate interactive meetings and conversations. Scheduling and joining meetings right from Teams streamlines collaboration. Screensharing and recording enable productivity.

The files tab allows central file storage for the team, like a cloud-based shared drive. Version history tracks changes and edits over time for documents. Great for collaboration.

Tabs like OneNote and Planner integrate Microsoft app capabilities right into your team workspace. Extensions also connect third-party apps like project management tools for centralized workflow.

Use the activity tab for an overview of recent interactions, mentions and updates across teams. Stay on top of tasks and conversations from one place. Enable notifications to stay informed.

Organize teams and channels using tabs for intuitive navigation. Favorite key contacts. Use @ tags in posts to link teams, channels and members for transparency.

Security and compliance tools allow controlling settings like guest access, password policies, data retention and legal holds. Admins can enable recording policies and permissions.

While learning Teams takes adjustment, its versatility can transform group communication and project management compared to email chains and phone calls. Embrace it for the next generation of teamwork.

Connecting and Sharing with Other Devices

One of Windows 11's strengths is its ecosystem of seamless connectivity between devices. You can easily link PCs, phones, tablets, displays, and other peripherals for integrated productivity and entertainment.

Connecting Windows and Android

A new Windows 11 feature is extensive integration with Android devices. You can link your Android phone to sync notifications, photos, apps, and more.

Enable this in Settings under Bluetooth & Devices > Linked devices. On your Android, download the Microsoft Link to Windows app from Google Play to set up pairing. Tap notifications from your phone right on your PC.

You can also install and run Android apps on Windows 11 devices thanks to Microsoft's collaboration with Amazon Appstore. This unifies your mobile and desktop worlds.

Linking to iOS Devices

While a bit more limited than Android integration, you can still connect your iPhone or iPad to Windows 11 primarily for seamless photo syncing.

Connect your iOS device with a cable or via Bluetooth. Open Photos app and enable syncing to pull your iPhone images into Windows for management, editing, and sharing.

This Photo sync option is tucked into Settings under Bluetooth & Devices. Turn it on and let your photo libraries stay up to date across devices.

Sharing with Wireless Displays

Wirelessly casting your Windows or Android screen onto TVs and displays is easy with Miracast support. Open the Connect panel and enable wireless projection to route your device screen to any supported display.

You can duplicate your display or only project certain windows while keeping your device screen private. Useful for presentations and viewing photos/videos from small screens on big screens.

Connecting Bluetooth Peripherals

You can pair Bluetooth headphones, speakers, game controllers, and other peripherals to your Windows 11 desktop with just a few clicks.

Open Settings > Bluetooth & Devices and switch Bluetooth On. Select "Add device" and put the gadget in pairing mode. Windows will automatically detect and connect it.

Reliable Bluetooth expands your Windows capabilities with wireless keyboards, mice, headsets, and controllers from any brand.

Network File Sharing

Link Windows PCs through your home network to share files and printers seamlessly. Use the Network pane in File Explorer to access public folders on other devices and share your own.

You can allow pin code access to private network shares for guests or more permanent networked access with Microsoft accounts. Right click folders to quickly share them across your LAN.

Integrating Windows devices into a unified productivity and entertainment ecosystem brings major quality of life benefits. Which connections matter most depend on your cross-device workflow and needs.

Using Cloud Services for Storage and Sharing

Cloud storage services provide convenient online access to your files from any device, and enables easy sharing. Top solutions like OneDrive, Dropbox, Google Drive and iCloud offer valuable capabilities for managing your digital library. We'll overview core features, best practices and integration to streamline productivity.

Cloud services host your files on remote servers, allowing access from your PC, smartphone and other logged-in devices. Edits sync across locations so versions stay updated universally. No more emailing files to yourself!

Most providers start you off with free storage space around 5-15GB, with paid monthly plans that expand capacity up to terabytes. Only store essential files in the cloud to conserve your limit.

Robust apps make accessing cloud files easy from your local device file explorer. Save files directly to the cloud folder for automatic syncing, or drag and drop existing files in. Open files also sync back any changes.

Leading services allow sharing files and folders via generated links or direct collaborator access. Securely grant editing rights and track activity. Great for collaboration and sending large attachments via simple shares.

Enable automatic photo and video backup from mobile devices for instant cloud archiving. Some services can recognize faces for smarter organization and searching based on who's present.

Two-factor authentication, encryption of data at rest and in transit, and other security measures protect cloud content from hacking and snooping. But minor risks still exist.

Additional convenience features vary by provider, like document creation and editing, website hosting, music storage, restore from malicious file removal, transfer tools and more. Explore offerings.

Integrations with Windows 11, Microsoft 365 and Chrome aim to embed cloud services for seamless productivity. Understand how each solution interacts with your workflows.

While embracing the cloud requires some adjustment, the benefits for accessibility, collaboration and assurance of off-site backup are immense. Cloud services unlock our digital potential.

CHAPTER 5

PERSONALIZATION AND ACCESSIBILITY

Personalizing Your Desktop

One of the best aspects of Windows is the ability to customize your desktop with visual flair and optimized efficiency. Personalizing the desktop allows you to change the look, layout, colors, sounds, and configuration to suit your style and needs. Let's explore desktop settings for customization.

Changing the Wallpaper

The wallpaper provides the backdrop for your desktop canvas. Windows 11 includes a gallery of beautiful included wallpaper images you can choose from.

Right click the desktop and select "Personalize" to access wallpaper options. Browse the dynamic and static images in various categories like landscapes, textures, art, and solid colors.

You can also use any personal photos and images as custom wallpaper. Right click an image file, select "Set as desktop background" and it will apply instantly.

Choosing an Accent Color

The accent color subtly applies to elements like Start menu tiles, window title bars, and buttons for a splash of color. Open Personalization settings and select "Colors" to pick your preferred accent color.

You can even make accents different on a per-app basis. For example, blue for File Explorer windows and red for Edge browser windows. Get creative with colors.

Enabling Dark Mode

Under Personalization > Colors, toggle the Dark mode switch to instantly invert the color scheme for a stylish, modern look. Dark mode can also reduce eye strain.

You have the ability to set Dark mode to turn on automatically based on sunrise/sunset or custom scheduled times. Or change it manually as desired on the fly.

Customizing the Lock Screen

Personalize the lock screen with background imagery and quick status widgets accessed whenever you wake your device from sleep.

Under Personalization, select Lock screen. Pick slideshow wallpaper, enable useful widgets like calendar, clock, notifications, and more. Make your lock screen uniquely yours.

Showing Desktop Icons

Desktop icon visibility is configurable from the Personalization menu. You can choose which shortcut icons like This PC, Recycle Bin, frequent folders, etc. appear on the desktop.

Show only what you actually use for a clean look. Or fill the desktop with handy file and folder shortcuts. Toggle these options in the Themes > Desktop icon settings menu.

Using Themes

Microsoft curates and distributes pre-configured Windows themes encompassing wallpapers, sounds, icons, mouse cursors, and color schemes for easy one-click personalization.

Open Themes under Personalization and browse an array of options for home, nature, travel, productivity, and other aesthetics. Download a theme and customize it further.

In summary, the desktop personalization settings empower you to craft a Windows environment perfect for your needs and style. Take time to explore and apply various customizations for a desktop you love using every day.

Adjusting Accessibility Settings

Optimizing accessibility settings helps remove barriers for users with limitations in vision, hearing, dexterity and cognition. Windows 11 provides customizable options to amplify usability. We'll explore key settings to enable so Windows works FOR you, regardless of challenges.

Under Settings > Accessibility, the main tools are organized by vision, hearing, mobility, neurodiversity and other categories. Use the "Recommended" section as a starting point based on your needs.

For low vision accessibility, options include narrator text reading, magnification, high contrast themes, font scaling, cursor sizing and color filters to reduce eye strain. Test combinations to determine what helps most.

Audio accommodations involve mono channel playback for single ear use, increasing volume beyond system limits, visual alerts for sounds, subtitle options and text reading speed. Configure based on your hearing needs.

Keyboard, mouse and touch modifications help navigate the system more easily if dealing with mobility limitations in hands and fingers. Adjust speed, taps, gestures and other behaviors.

Focus assist tools reduce distractions by tinting other screens, limiting notifications and redirecting concentration during tasks. Essential to manage attention deficits.

The learning tools area centralizes reading and writing assists like dictation, constructing words by syllables, text suggestions during typing, synonym options and letter spacing configurations. Enable as required.

Administrative settings allow enabling ease of access tools during initial computer setup. Toggle high contrast or narrator before the operating system is fully loaded. A convenient head start.

Don't hesitate to test out different combinations of settings to find your optimal configuration. Conditions vary day to day. Keep fine tuning Windows to amplify capabilities and reduce frustrations.

The journey towards digital accessibility requires patience and a commitment to finding solutions. But persisting pays off in an empowered, customized Windows 11 experience that works for you, not against you. The path ahead comes into view.

Using Speech Recognition and Cortana

Windows 11 offers robust built-in speech recognition capabilities for voice typing and controlling your PC. The integrated Cortana digital assistant takes voice commands to manage tasks and information. Speech recognition enables operating your device hands-free, while Cortana amplifies productivity.

Enabling Speech Recognition

You can dictate text into any app using just your voice. Under Start > Settings > Time & Language, scroll to "Speech" and toggle the Speech recognition switch. Complete quick voice training.

Now in any text field, select a microphone icon or press Windows key + H to start dictating. Speak naturally to type hands-free. Punctuate with commands like "new line" or "new paragraph."

Improving Recognition Accuracy

For optimal accuracy, complete voice training under Speech settings. Train in a quiet environment using clear enunciation. Test recognition in a supported app like Word.

You can select words and correct mistranscriptions after dictating to further improve accuracy over time as the system learns your unique voice.

Using Dictation Mode

Enable Dictation mode from Speech settings for a dedicated voice typing experience. Launch Dictation mode then speak continuously as text appears.

Use verbal commands to format, select text, insert punctuation, capitalize words, etc. This dedicated mode gives you full voice control over typing.

Controlling Windows with Voice

Under Speech settings, enable "Voice activation" to control basic Windows navigation hands-free. Record wake words like "Computer" to trigger listening.

Now you can launch apps, switch windows, open menus, click buttons, scroll, and more using voice commands. Customize commands as needed for your preferred workflow.

Introduction to Cortana

Cortana is the personal digital assistant built into Windows 11. You can chat with Cortana conversationally to get information, set reminders, open apps, adjust settings, and automate tasks through voice commands and responses.

Access Cortana by clicking its taskbar icon or saying your wake phrase. Grant necessary permissions so Cortana can respond contextually based on your Microsoft account profile and activity history.

Getting Help from Cortana

Pose questions conversationally to Cortana like "How's the weather today?" or "What's on my calendar?" to get quick answers without typing.

Cortana taps into Bing search to supply definitions, calculations, translations, facts, news, and other information visually or through speech. Leverage its knowledge hands-free.

Managing Tasks with Cortana

Request Cortana to set reminders, alarms, calendar appointments, and lists. Say things like "Remind me to call Mom at 6 PM." Cortana will record tasks you can review in the Cortana pane.

Use Cortana to set up routines like playing music when you arrive home. Or have it mute notifications when you enter fullscreen apps to minimize distractions when you need to focus.

In summary, speech recognition and Cortana enable controlling Windows 11 devices completely hands-free using just your voice. Dictate text, launch apps, get information, automate tasks, and more with these convenient built-in tools.

Setting Up Printers and Other External Devices

Connecting printers, scanners, external drives and other peripheral devices expands what you can achieve with your Windows 11 PC.

Most printers connect via Wi-Fi for wireless printing, or a USB cable for wired operation. Follow device-specific instructions for installation like CD software or downloading drivers from the manufacturer's website based on your model.

Under Settings > Bluetooth & Devices, you can add a new printer or scanner by selecting it from discovered nearby devices if Bluetooth enabled. The system should automatically install any required software drivers.

For older printer models, you may need to manually select the port, model and driver from the vendor's options during installation for proper connectivity. Familiarize yourself with the printer properties.

Adjust default printer options like print quality, paper size and tray settings based on your typical usage. Customize maintenance options for sleep schedules and ink levels to safeguard operation.

Scanners require calibrating color balance, resolution, file format and destination folder settings to ensure accurate document digitization. Run test scans to check for quality.

External backup drives should be high capacity but affordable, and connect via USB, wireless or external power as needed. Schedule regular file history backups or system image archives.

Carefully eject hardware like flash drives, hard drives and other external storage devices using the safe removal icon before unplugging to avoid file transfer issues or corruption.

Troubleshoot printer issues by checking cable connections, power cycle the device, inspect paper levels/jams, reinstall drivers, update firmware, use cleaning tools, adjust configurations in printer properties and consult manufacturer support articles before assuming failure.

Maintain printers through regular cleaning, alignment checks, nozzle purges and test prints to sustain print quality over time. Proper upkeep prevents many problems.

Patience and methodical troubleshooting keep peripherals performing smoothly. But don't hesitate to contact vendor tech support if problems persist. Take advantage of included warranties and service periods to maximize value.

Using Windows 11's Ease of Access Features

Windows 11 provides customizable accessibility features to make using your computer more manageable for those managing limitations in vision, hearing, mobility or cognition. Optimizing these settings removes barriers and amplifies capabilities. We'll explore key options for magnifying, narrating, modifying inputs and focusing attention to transform accessibility.

Under Settings > Accessibility, the main ease of access tools are organized by vision, hearing, mobility, neurodiversity and other categories. The "Recommended" section suggests options based on your usage patterns and noted challenges.

For low vision users, options include screen narration, magnification, high contrast themes, increasing text and icon sizing, customizing cursor and focus visuals, adjusting color filters and enabling friendly font faces like Comic Sans.

Audio accommodations involve mono channel support, increasing volume beyond system limits, enabling visual alerts for app sounds, customizing subtitle presentation and speeding up/slowing down narrator text reading rates.

Keyboard, mouse and touch modifications assist by adjusting tap sensitivity, ignoring repeated inputs, modifying scroll/zoom behaviors, toggling click lock and accessing hover text via touches instead of mouse hovers.

Focus assist tools aim to help maintain attention by tinting other screens while in an app, limiting distracting notifications and system sounds, and redirecting concentration when needed.

Learning tools provide text predictions during typing, read aloud options, construct words by syllables, picture dictionaries for vocabulary aid, grammar and spacing settings for dyslexia and tools to navigate by headings or excerpt sentences.

Administrative settings allow enabling accessibility options like narrator and high contrast during initial computer setup before Windows is fully loaded to get started immediately.

Don't hesitate to test different combinations of settings to determine your ideal configuration. Sensory and cognitive needs vary day to day, so regularly reassess tools for their utility. Consistent adjustments keep systems supportive over time as abilities evolve. With the right settings, Windows 11 can help you accomplish more on your own terms. Accessibility opens doors to independence.

CHAPTER 6

SECURITY AND MAINTENANCE

Understanding Windows 11 Security Features

With continuous enhancements across the board, Windows 11 provides stronger security protections than ever before against modern digital threats. Robust antivirus tools, encryption, firewalls, biometric authentication, and core isolation combine to create a hardened OS.

Microsoft Defender Antivirus

This built-in antivirus solution provides comprehensive real-time scanning, threat detection, removal, and quarantining to stop malware infections. Enable it under Settings > Privacy & Security > Windows Security for robust protection.

Defender constantly monitors system activity across email, downloads, apps, browsers, files, and network connections to identify and block potential threats before they can compromise your PC. Schedule regular scans for full coverage.

Windows Firewall

Also managed under Windows Security, Firewall provides a shield against unauthorized network access and connections. Enable it to hide your PC from prying eyes and block incoming malicious connections.

Firewall allows trusted apps internet access while restricting suspicious programs. Further lock things down by disabling unneeded port and network permissions that could expose your system to exploits.

BitLocker Drive Encryption

This feature fully encrypts internal and external drives at the volume level to secure data from physical theft. Even if a drive is removed, connecting it elsewhere will require entering the encryption key to unlock it.

Manage BitLocker under Settings > System > Storage to enable and configure on your system drive and external storage devices like USB drives. This renders data inaccessible without the key.

Windows Hello Biometric Sign In

Forget typing passwords! Windows Hello enables signing into Windows 11 using fingerprint readers, facial recognition through compatible webcams, or PINs.

Set this up under Settings > Accounts > Sign-in options to register your identity. Now just scan your fingerprint or face to authenticate without passwords. More secure and convenient.

Virtualization Based Security

This enterprise-grade protection isolates critical system processes like the kernel, antivirus, encryption, and credential guard in a separate virtual environment safe from malware tampering.

With regulated access, exploits are much harder to leverage even through vulnerabilities. Virtualization based security is enabled by default to further harden systems.

Tracking Prevention

Under Settings > Privacy & Security > Privacy, enable the various options for preventing apps and services from monitoring your activity across Windows and web browsing. This enhances privacy.

Options like limiting background apps, toggling diagnostics and tailored experiences, and controlling tracking permissions give you granular control over data sharing you're uncomfortable with.

Overall, while no solution is impenetrable, Windows 11 checks all the boxes for core security protections backed by ongoing research and development from Microsoft. Enable key features for peace of mind.

Protecting Your PC from Viruses and Malware

Safeguarding your computer against malicious software threats like viruses, spyware, ransomware and hackers represents a fundamental priority for all users. Practicing prudent online precautions, enabling key security tools and monitoring for warning signs proactively defends your system. We'll cover essential antivirus and malware protection principles to help secure your digital life.

The most vital defense is common sense - avoiding suspicious links, unrecognized attachments, pirated software and sketchy websites limits exposure opportunities tremendously. If something seems questionable, don't chance it. Err on the side of caution always.

Use reputable antivirus software with real-time protection capabilities and schedule regular system scans. Windows Security provides strong basics, while third party programs like Malwarebytes add robust layers. Enable auto-quarantine as well.

Firewall settings on your router and locally on your Windows Security app monitor network traffic and block potentially malicious connections. Turn these on to hide your PC from random probes.

Regular system updates for Windows and Office close security loopholes and bugs as discovered. Enable automatic updates for convenience and compliance. Updates inconvenience us temporarily to protect us permanently.

Cryptolocker attacks that encrypt files and demand ransom originate from malicious links or attachments. Maintain offline backups via external drives to recover data in this emergency situation. Avoid paying ransoms.

Monitor task manager occasionally for unknown processes hogging resources, which could indicate malware. Research unfamiliar programs installed to verify legitimacy and origin.

Wiping and reloading Windows is an option if malware becomes severe enough. Backup personal files first locally, then perform a clean reset. Use this nuclear option cautiously.

Concerning passwords, enable MFA, use a password manager, avoid repeats and dictionary words. Rotate frequently, use maximum length, and delete unused logins. Strong passwords frustrate hackers.

Overall, prudent precautions minimize malware significantly. But no system is impenetrable. Staying vigilant to risks, monitoring for uncommon issues and consistently applying security protocols helps safeguard your digital life. Peace of mind is priceless.

Regular System Maintenance and Updates

Over time, all computers accumulate clutter and suffer performance degradation without proper care. Practicing consistent system maintenance preserves Windows 11 speed, stability, and security. From software updates to storage organization, establishing good maintenance habits is essential.

Installing Updates

Always keep Windows, drivers, firmware, and applications fully updated by promptly installing available updates when notified. Updates patch bugs, close security holes, and bring new features.

Open Settings > Windows Update and click "Check for updates" to manually check. Restart when prompted after installing updates and allow time for changes to finalize. Enable automatic updates for convenience.

Updating prevents technical debt from accumulating and leading to problems down the road. Stay current and reap the continuous improvements.

Disk Cleanup

Disk Cleanup frees wasted hard drive space by safely removing temporary files, downloads, system logs, caches, and other unneeded fluff occupying storage. Open it under Settings > System > Storage.

Check all categories then click "Clean up system files" to reclaim significant space. Set it to run automatically on a schedule for convenience. Keeping your disks lean improves performance.

UninstallingUnused Programs

Get rid of apps and software you no longer need by uninstalling them through Settings > Apps > Installed apps. This prevents them from launching at boot, updating, and occupying storage space unnecessarily.

Sort apps by last used date and remove obsolete ones. Avoid residual clutter by cleaning up unneeded software cruft periodically.

Clearing Browser Data

Web browsers cache visited sites, cookies, history, and other temporary usage data that builds up steadily, slowing things down. Clear this data manually through your browser's settings/privacy menu.

Set browsers to automatically delete privacy data like cookies/history after each session for improved speed and privacy. Keep cache clearing on a monthly schedule for optimal browser performance.

Backing Up Files

Protect irreplaceable documents and media by maintaining both local and cloud backups that safeguard your data from hardware failures, theft, and ransomware. Use external drives and cloud storage.

Configure regular file history or file backup schedules to automate copying important folders like Documents, Pictures, Desktop, and Downloads to external drives periodically. Supplement with cloud storage like OneDrive.

Resetting Default Apps

Over time, you may accumulate numerous unnecessary default app associations that clutter the system and cause conflicts. Reset defaults under Settings > Apps > Default apps to restore order.

This lets you specify your preferred browser, media player, email client and other defaults. Remove unused apps as options to prevent system clutter.

Formatting and Partitioning

For fresh devices or a full system refresh, reformatting the hard drive and repartitioning storage optimally erases bloat and provides a clean slate. Use the Disk Management utility to format and set up partitions from scratch.

Start with a clean C: OS partition, add a D: data partition, and allocate the rest as shared storage. This structures everything logically from the ground up.

Consistently maintaining your Windows PC gives you the best computing experience possible. Make habits of these tips and enjoy smooth system performance for many years.

Backing Up and Restoring Your System

Protecting your files and settings with regular backups enables recovering from catastrophic failures, malicious attacks and unintended deletions. We'll explore backup methods, what to include, ideal schedules and restoration best practices. Embracing robust backup protocols safeguards your digital life.

Windows includes built-in tools like File History for automated document backups to external drives, and system image creation via Macrium Reflect for full system snapshots. Use both for comprehensive coverage.

File History continually saves versions of files in selected folders like Documents, Pictures and Desktop. Let it run automatically once configured for perpetual protection.

System image backups require periodic manual creation, but capture the entire operating system state including programs and settings. Retain at least 3 generations locally.

For external backup drives, aim for at least 1TB capacity, USB 3.0 speeds, and portability if wanted for off-site storage. Schedule monthly images, with interim file backups.

Backup priorities include personal files and folders first, installed software and drivers if bandwidth allows, media like photos and videos lastly. Focus on irreplaceable data.

Store one backup copy locally like an external drive, and ideally one remote like a cloud service for redundancy against local disasters like fires or floods. Diversify storage.

Test backups by deliberately deleting a file, then attempting restore. Verify backups run on schedule via reports. Catch issues early, backups are useless if faulty.

To recover lost files, use File History's timeline view to find versions prior to deletion and restore. For system disasters, boot from the external image copy fully.

Patience is key – retreating to an earlier version or rebuild takes time and applications may need reinstalling. But prevailing is worth the hassle for data preserved.

With a disciplined backup routine for both files and full systems, worst case scenarios become just inconvenient setbacks, not catastrophic loss. Backup diligently and rest assured.

Troubleshooting Common Issues

Despite Windows 11's reliability, occasional issues can still arise that require troubleshooting. Problems like slow performance, crashes, audio problems, or Wi-Fi connectivity can be frustrating. Thankfully, many basic troubleshooting steps can resolve common issues and get your PC running smoothly again.

Troubleshooting Slow Performance

Over time, PCs inevitably accumulate clutter leading to sluggish performance. If your computer feels slow, try these troubleshooting steps:

- Close unused programs and browser tabs to free up RAM
- Disable startup programs you don't need
- Run Disk Cleanup to remove temporary files and system clutter
- Update Windows, drivers, and apps to fix bugs slowing you down
- Open Task Manager and end background processes hogging resources
- Reboot your computer for a fresh start after busy sessions

Following general performance best practices helps avoid sluggishness in the first place. But when slowdowns strike, this checklist can optimize your system.

Resolving App Crashes

Random app crashes can stem from buggy software, outdated drivers, system file corruption, or hardware problems like bad RAM. Try these fixes for unstable apps:

- Update the app and graphics/chipset drivers to the latest version
- Use System File Checker to scan for corrupted files and restore integrity
- Toggle hardware acceleration options in app settings if available
- Uninstall and reinstall the crashing application
- Restart computer to eliminate transient software issues
- Check memory diagnostics for RAM issues causing crashes

With trial and error, you can isolate the cause of unstable apps. Don't hesitate to contact the developer for further support if crashes persist.

Fixing Audio Issues

Problems like no audio, static, or distortion often arise from driver conflicts or incorrect default devices selected. To resolve:

- Open Sound settings to confirm correct input/output devices are enabled
- Update audio drivers from manufacturer or Windows Update
- Disable unused audio devices to prevent conflicts
- Restart audio services and processes via Task Manager
- In apps, reselect preferred output device in audio options
- Reset PRAM/NVRAM on Mac systems to clear audio config settings

With a bit of tweaking, you can pinpoint and resolve the cause of pesky audio issues.

Troubleshooting Network Connectivity

Sluggish internet or connection problems can occur from router configuration issues, bandwidth bottlenecks, or device limitations. Try these steps:

- Reboot the router and your device to refresh connections
- Ensure Wi-Fi drivers are updated on your machine
- Move closer to the router or access point for a stronger signal
- Reset network adapters under Device Manager
- Disable bandwidth hogging apps and devices if speeds improve
- Check ISP for regional outages if web access is fully down

Confirm basic connectivity first, then tweak your network setup for maximum speeds. Contact your ISP if problems persist across devices.

Recovering From Crashes

In worst case scenarios like an unbootable system after a crash, recovery options include:

- Booting into Safe Mode via startup settings to troubleshoot issues

- Using System Restore to revert to a previous working restore point
- Running chkdsk to check and repair drive errors
- Restoring from a system image backup
- Performing an in-place upgrade repair install
- Clean reinstalling Windows as a last resort

With Windows 11's reliability improvements, total crashes are rare. But serious problems can still occur, so understanding recovery procedures is crucial for getting up and running again.

By methodically applying appropriate troubleshooting techniques, many common issues are easily resolvable. Arm yourself with this knowledge to tackle problems efficiently as they arise.

CHAPTER 7

EXPLORING FURTHER

Introduction to Microsoft Office Suite

Microsoft Office represents the premier suite of productivity applications for documents, spreadsheets, presentations and more. Learning to navigate its core word processing, calculation, and slideshow tools enables creating professional content seamlessly. We'll get started with the essentials in Word, Excel and PowerPoint.

Word facilitates professional document creation and editing. Templates streamline formatting reports, letters, resumes and more. Review tab tools allow collaborative review cycles and commentary between authors. Tables and images incorporate easily.

Excel models data for analysis and calculations in grid-based worksheets using formulas and functions. PivotTables dynamically filter, summarize and present data insights. Charts visualize the spreadsheet numerically. Automation boosts efficiency.

PowerPoint enables developing engaging multimedia presentations using slides, animations and transitions. Themes and layouts produce polished results effortlessly. Presenter view simplifies delivering shows.

Across apps, the ribbon interface organizes commands by task for intuitive navigation. Contextual tabs surface options related to selected items. Quick Access condenses common functions. Learning ribbons accelerates mastery.

Keyboard shortcuts, right-click menus and touch gestures offer alternative access to features for power users. Enabling the Editor pane surfaces formatting marks for polished results.

Office integrates with cloud storage for accessing files across devices. AutoSave and version history reduce risk of lost work. Share content digitally via OneDrive or email with recipients.

For beginners, focus on competency in Word and PowerPoint first for foundational literacy. Excel scales in complexity and benefits from deliberate learning of formulas, datasets and charting to maximize capabilities.

Embrace templates and sample files to kickstart your designs rather than starting completely from scratch. Customizing prebuilt content is faster for polished results.

While mastering Office takes time, perseverance pays dividends in amplified productivity and professional aptitude. Let the tools handle tedious tasks so you can focus on big picture goals and creativity.

Using Windows Store to Download Apps and Games

The Windows Store provides a centralized hub to browse, purchase and install apps to enhance functionality and enjoyment on your Windows 11 device. Learning to leverage the store streamlines discovering new programs, games and tools from trusted developers. We'll tour the store's key sections and outline best practices.

The main Store interface highlights featured apps and games, top charts and categories like productivity, finance, health & fitness, music, reading, travel and more to inspire browsing. Search by keywords or scroll through selections.

Product pages detail version history, ratings, screenshots, descriptions and publisher info to evaluate quality and fit. Download button initiates installation. Manage and share apps from Library.

Gaming hub spotlights new releases, top grossing and highest rated titles across genres. PC gaming capabilities continue growing via Windows, so the Store provides convenient access to leading games.

Movies & TV hub enables purchasing or renting movies, TV shows and even streaming subscription channels. Digital content integrates across Windows 11 for enjoyment.

Before downloading apps, verify publisher reputation and review ratings/feedback for red flags about bugs, hidden fees or privacy concerns. Stick to known, trusted developers.

Use built-in antivirus scanning and enable app reputation checks in Windows Security to identify risky software. Safely test new apps in Sandbox mode first if uncertain.

Limit use of unnecessary apps to conserve disk space, memory usage and avoid background processes. Uninstall unused apps occasionally to clean up clutter.

For quality assurance, provide app feedback via reviews and utilize integrated reporting tools if issues arise for refund consideration. Help improve the ecosystem.

Overall, judiciously leveraging Windows Store to expand your app and game library in a secure manner enables safely enhancing capabilities and entertainment on Windows 11. Just remember to apply common sense and caution.

Basic Photo Editing with Microsoft Photos

The Microsoft Photos app provides capable photo management and editing tools right within Windows 11. From collections to enhancements, Photos empowers you to organize, personalize, and perfect your picture library.

Importing Photos

Start by importing images into Photos from folders on your PC like Documents or Downloads using the Import option.

You can also set up automated folder imports under Settings > Sources by enabling "Pictures folder" or adding custom folders to automatically sync new content. This prevents managing duplicates across locations.

Photos also pulls pictures from OneDrive, connected cameras, and social media if configured under Settings > Sources. Consolidate your photo collection for unified access and editing.

Cropping and Rotating

Common basic adjustments include cropping to key areas of interest and rotating to correct orientation.

Open a photo, then click Edit to access essentials like Cropping and Rotate tools. Drag your desired crop area, tweak the shape and size, then click Apply to finalize the change. Rotate in 90° increments as needed.

These quick tweaks refine composition and provide a cleaner focus on photo subjects without extraneous elements.

Tuning Lighting

Lighting improvements help brighten dark shots or tame overexposed ones. Under Edit, choose Adjustments then drag sliders for Exposure, Contrast, Highlights, Shadows and more to tune lighting.

Boost shadows to reveal details and lower highlights that are washed out. Increase contrast for more "pop". Photos makes lighting edits easy.

Boosting Color and Clarity

Similarly, adjust Color and Clarity sliders within Adjustments to improve the vibrancy and sharpness of your photos.

Bump Saturation and Vibrance to intensify colors without distorting skin tones. Increase Clarity to add midtone contrast for more vivid depth without oversharpening.

These quick tweaks really make photos pop for sharing and can turn mundane pictures into something special.

Applying Filters

For fun effects, explore the Filters tab like Dramatic, Vintage, Elegant and Monochrome. Filters apply preset color/tone changes.

Double click a filter thumbnail to preview, then click Apply to commit it non-destructively to the image. Change or remove filters anytime without losing original photo data.

Play around with filters to imbue photos with different moods. But use them sparingly and subtly for best results.

Removing Red Eye

A common portrait problem, red eye happens when a camera flash reflects in people's retinas. Thankfully the Red Eye tool makes it simple to correct.

Just click Edit then Red Eye. Zoom into each affected eye, click within it, and redness is automatically removed. Minimize this distracting effect with ease.

Retouching and Blurring

Under Edit, the Retouch tool lets you paint over and blend away blemishes, dust spots, power lines or other small distractions, for portrait glamour shots or cleaner landscape photos.

For artful background blur, click Select > Subject to intelligently select the foreground person/object then apply Gaussian Blur to aesthetically separate them from backgrounds.

Photos empowers anyone to dive in and refine photos through easy editing options. Don't hesitate to explore and tailor the editing experience under Settings > Editing as well. With practice, you'll achieve stunning results from even average photos!

Enjoying Music and Videos with Media Player

The refined Media Player app provides a centralized hub for enjoying your music and video collections on Windows 11. With intuitive design and handy organizational tools, Media Player makes personal media streaming fun and accessible.

Importing Your Music Library

To access your tunes in Media Player, first import your music folders and files. Click Manage Library > Music > Add folders and select folders like Documents/Music to index them.

Imported tracks appear in a Recently added section for quick access. Media Player also links to Microsoft Groove Music streaming if you have a subscription.

Organizing Music into Playlists

Create custom playlists to neatly organize songs by mood, genre, decade or any theme. Make one on the fly by dragging songs into a new playlist folder in the sidebar. Rearrange tracks via drag-and-drop within playlists.

For regular playlists like workout music or favorites, enable Sync this playlist for offline access under playlist options. Building playlists helps match tunes to activities.

Improving Music Playback

Adjust Playback settings from the Now Playing toolbar like crossfade, enhancements like graphic equalizer and spatial sound, playback speed, and visualization during music playback.

Enable Lyrics view to sing along during playback. Extend these options on a per-device basis like exclusive spatial audio for headphones vs. stereo speakers.

Importing and Streaming Video

You can populate Media Player with home movies and other video files the same way as music - via folder import in Manage Library. Imported videos appear in the Recent section.

Alternatively, link streaming services like Amazon Prime Video, Hulu, or YouTube via Apps in the sidebar for access within Media Player for consolidated viewing.

Managing Videos

Unlike music, the Media Player video library automatically sorts content into Home videos and Other videos categories for quick access. Can also view by Date added or Name.

Open metadata details to edit video titles, dates, artwork and related organizational details. Add descriptive tags like family, vacation, etc to make searching easier with larger libraries.

Optimizing Video Playback

Adjust settings during video playback via the Now Playing toolbar like subtitles, audio track preferences, zoom, video enhancers like sharper image, and always playing audio on your default speakers.

Enable Cinema mode for a cinematic letterbox view. Extend playback with paired Bluetooth speakers or Xbox consoles. Tweak settings to optimize enjoyment.

Creating Playlists and Mixes

Craft custom video playlists by manually adding desired videos to a new playlist folder just like songs above. Perfect for curating exercise videos, kids' cartoons, highlight reels and more.

You can also generate automatic playlists based on criteria like genre, year, or keyword tags. Dynamic mixes keep listening and viewing fresh.

With intuitive tools for managing libraries, generating playlists, and customizing playback, Media Player provides a feature-packed entertainment hub suited to music and video aficionados.

Closing Remarks and Next Steps

After digesting the core topics presented in this guide, you should have a foundational yet thorough understanding of using and optimizing Windows 11 for productivity and entertainment. This final chapter recaps key takeaways and recommends resources for further developing your skills.

Revisiting Key Concepts

Let's briefly revisit some of the most important concepts from core chapters:

- The Start menu organizes access to apps, files, and system settings. Pin your most-used items for convenience.

- The Taskbar contains apps, search, system tray, widgets panel, and virtual desktops access. Customize pinned items and behavior.

- File Explorer enables navigating, opening, organizing, and managing files, applications, storage drives, networks, and clouds.

- Microsoft Edge provides fast, secure web browsing. Use built-in tools like Collections and Read Aloud to enhance your workflow.

- Windows Security protects against malware and network intrusions with antivirus, firewall, and threat prevention tools. Keep protections active.

- System maintenance like updates, drive optimization, backups, and performance monitoring keeps Windows running smoothly long-term.

- Accessibility features allow using Windows your way including text resizing, visual aids, captions, voice dictation, and more.

These concepts establish a strong foundation. Now let's look at some resources to build upon this base.

Expanding Your Knowledge

The best way to master Windows is consistent, daily usage to ingrain habits and workflows. But supplemental learning resources can accelerate the process:

- Microsoft Support articles and walkthroughs provide task-focused guidance. Browse help content or search for your issue.

- Digital training courses like LinkedIn Learning offer video lessons on Windows topics for visual learners.

- The Microsoft Tips app delivers bite-sized tutorials for daily competence boosts right on your PC.

- IT communities like Reddit offer opportunities to ask questions and learn from other Windows power users.

- Printed guidebooks provide structured learning pathways if you prefer tactile reading.

Don't hesitate to employ search engines to find solutions to everyday usage questions. The digital library is endless - tap into it!

Exploring New Windows 11 Capabilities

Looking ahead, Windows 11 will continue evolving with major updates. Stay on top of new features and apps that can boost your productivity:

- Enhanced touchscreen and stylus support creates a great tablet experience.

- WSL 2 propels development by running Linux directly within Windows.

- Gaming improvements like Auto HDR and DirectStorage optimize performance.

- Widgets on the personalized feed screen provide at-a-glance info.

- Seamless Android app integration bridges mobile ecosystems.

Upgrading to new hardware and peripherals can also unlock capabilities. There's always more to learn with Windows!

The Journey Continues

Understanding Windows 11 is an ongoing process, but you now have the essentials for everyday usage. Continue perfecting your skills and watch your confidence and proficiency grow.

This guide aimed to help you use Windows in an empowered way. We hope the concepts within provide a gateway to improved productivity and enjoyment.

Here's wishing you expert-level Windows mastery fueled by consistent usage and continual learning! Your journey continues...

BONUS 1

AUDIOBOOK

Scan the QR code and listen to the audiobook

Toni Davison

BONUS 2

VIDEO

Scan the QR code

Toni Davison

EXCLUSIVE BONUS

3 EBOOK

Scan the QR code or click the link and access the bonuses

http://subscribepage.io/AcMzyi

AUTHOR BIO
TONI DAVISON

Toni Davison, an accomplished author and software expert deeply entrenched in the realm of computer science. Toni's journey commenced in the digital arena as a young enthusiast, navigating the evolving landscape of information technology.

By day, Toni emerges as a seasoned professional in software development, dedicating decades to mastering the intricacies of coding, algorithms, and emerging technologies. His expertise spans various programming languages and software frameworks, establishing him as a respected figure in the ever-expanding field of computer science.

Toni's journey is characterized by a commitment to continuous learning, staying abreast of the latest advancements to offer practical insights to both novices and seasoned professionals. Beyond the lines of code, he is a problem solver, channeling his analytical skills to create innovative solutions that bridge the gap between theory and real-world application.

In addition to his role as a software expert, Toni is a passionate advocate for digital literacy, empowering individuals to navigate the complexities of the digital age.